ELEPHANTS IN THE NEWS

PACHYDERMS IN LIMERICK

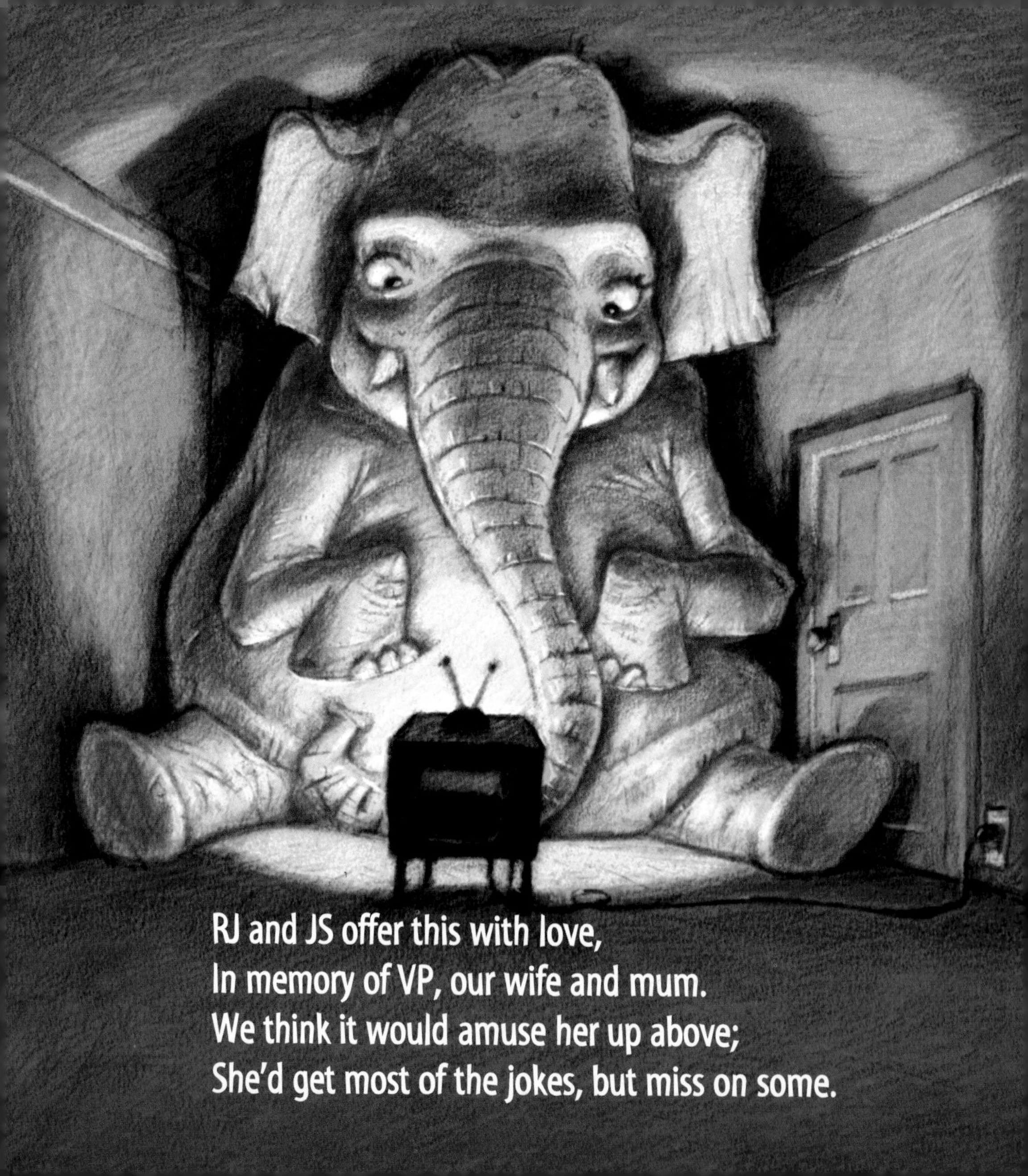

RJ and JS offer this with love,
In memory of VP, our wife and mum.
We think it would amuse her up above;
She'd get most of the jokes, but miss on some.

ELEPHANTS IN THE NEWS

PACHYDERMS IN LIMERICK

limericks by R.J. BAKER

illustrations by J.S. BAKER

inspired by ADA CHEUNG

EXISLE
PUBLISHING

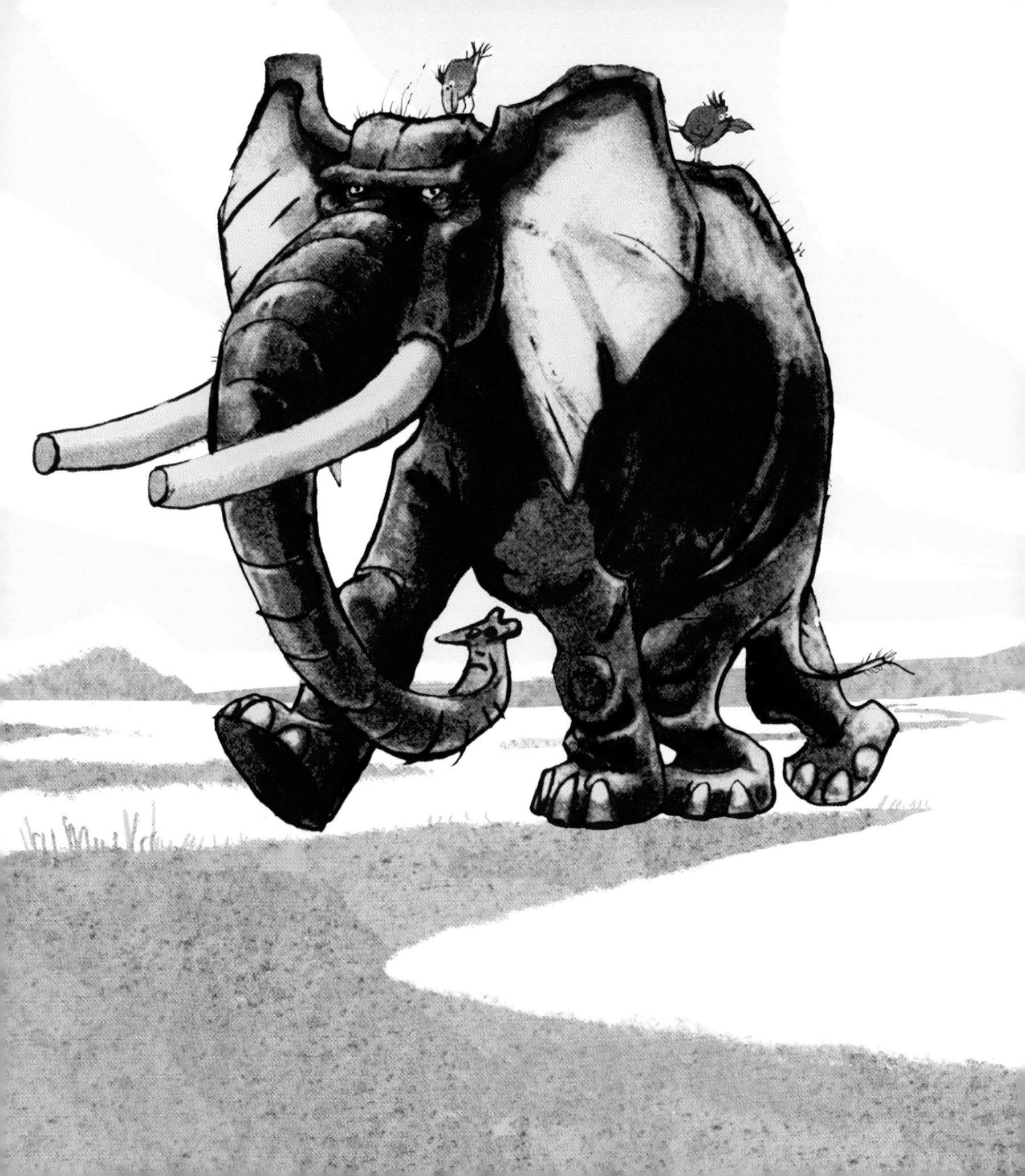

CONTENTS

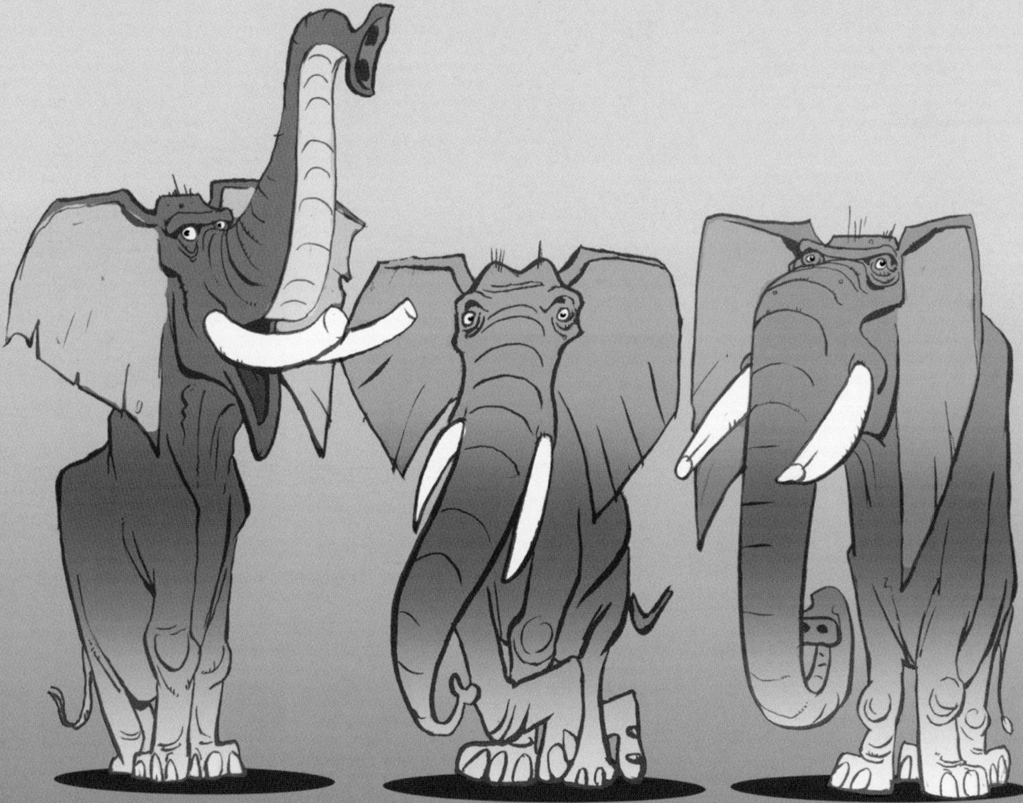

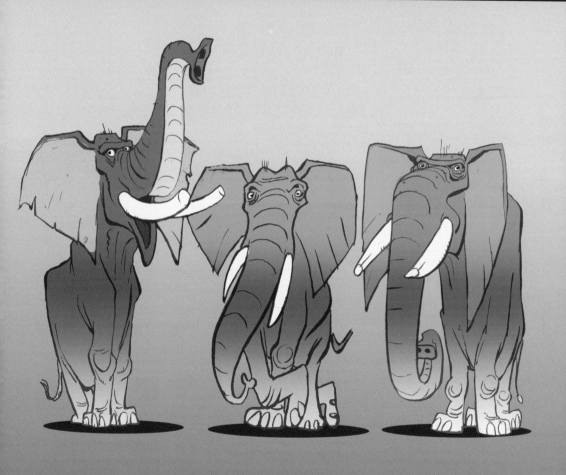

FOREWORD

What do you get if you combine a Classicist with a rare talent for translating Latin verse, a news-mad tutor, and a professional illustrator who happens to be the son of the first? Well, if the stars and planets align, as they once did over the University of New England in Australia, the answer — eventually — is a book of illustrated limericks.

Allow me to explain. In the then Department of Classics and Ancient History, the downstairs corridor, where Rob's office was, was affectionately known as the Tuskers' Graveyard. This in-joke was firmly part of the departmental culture by 1997, when a newly hatched baby academic for a semester was warmly adopted by the tuskers, who took me under their collective trunks, so to speak.

Now, one of Rob's specialities is replicating the metres of Latin verse in English, in a double-whammy feat of translation. A side-effect is an astounding facility with limericks, often piqued by current events; a series on the Prince and Princess of Wales (I hasten to add this predated a certain car crash) won a national newspaper competition.

Given that I already maintained a customised newswire service, sending articles from on-line papers to friends and colleagues according to their interests, it was inevitable that Wonce Wozza, the eponymous Muse of the Limerick, dictated that elephants in the news should be directed to Rob. These exchanges incited a series of occasional verses which continued for years, outlasting any number of personal and professional metamorphoses.

After Rob realised that we had more than enough material for a booklet, he co-opted his son James to provide the necessary illustrative input to round out the project.

So that's the story — and we're sticking to it. Private jokes are rarely amusing to those who weren't there at the time, but we trust that this is an exception.

As Wonce Wozza's most devoted disciple, Anon, put it:

The limerick's an art form complex
Whose contents run mainly to sex.
It's famous for virgins and masculine urgin's,
And vulgar erotic effects.

And elephants.

Ada Cheung
Canberra

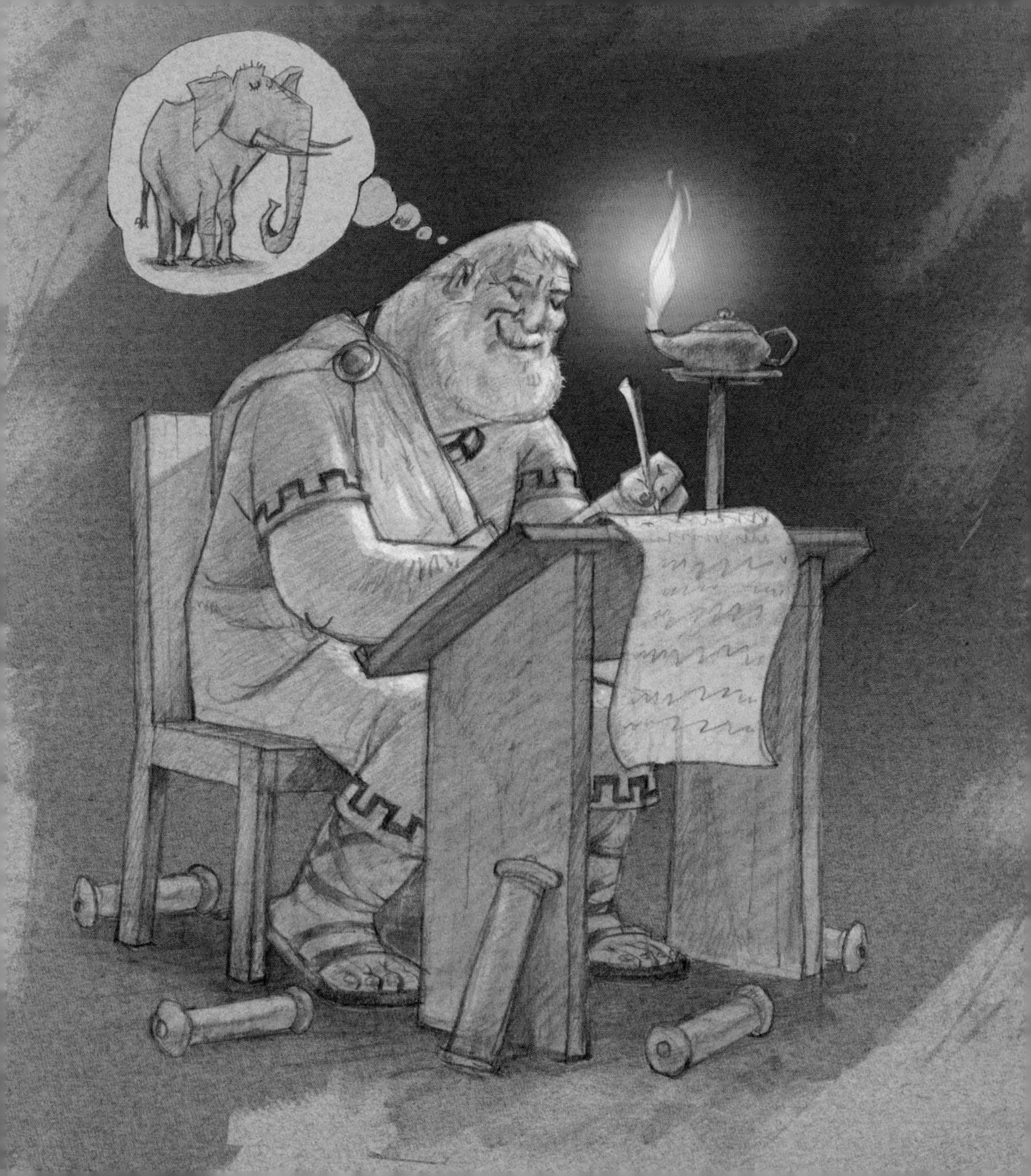

INTRODUCTION

maximum est elephans proximumque humanis sensibus, quippe intellectus illis sermonis patrii et imperiorum obedientia, officiorum quae didicere memoria, amoris et gloriae voluptas, immo vero quae etiam in homine rara: probitas, prudentia, aequitas.

Pliny the Elder, *Naturalis Historia*, VIII.1

The largest [sc. among land animals] is the elephant and the closest to human intelligence. For they have understanding of their country's speech and are obedient to commands, remember tasks which they have learned, and take pleasure in affection and marks of honour. Nay more, they have qualities which even in man are rare: honesty, foresight and fairness.

Old texts hadn't made me a dimmer stick.
Ada's news items started to glimmer quick:
As each item came,
I would set out to frame
A commentary couched in a limerick.

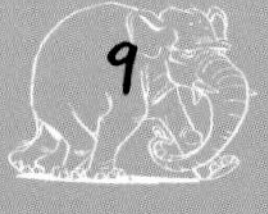

World-wide was the field of our questing
For elephant news; always testing
   Their hopes, fears, and dealings
    With life — all their feelings,
Our zeal neither flagging nor resting.

        To keep readers much wide-awaker,
        The art work (a laughter up-shaker!)
           Will lighten the text
           Of poor elephants vexed;
        My eldest son's work, James S. Baker.

In circus, on plains, or in zoos,
No matter what yardstick you choose,
   Come work, strife or play,
    At the end of the day
Those elephants always are news.

CHAPTER ONE:
ELEPHANTS IN SCIENCE

The elephants rumbled defiance:
'We pachyderms don't owe compliance
   To shibboleths old.
   In fact, I'd make bold
To say we're devoted to science.'

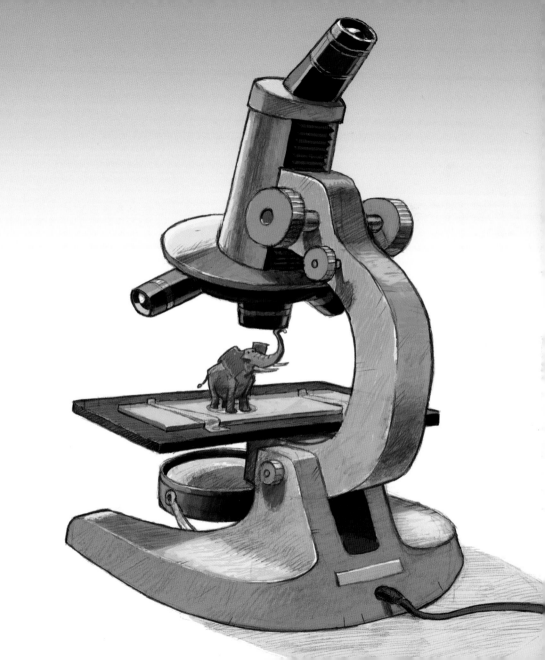

GENES REVEAL AFRICA'S ELEPHANTS AS TWO SEPARATE SPECIES

Africa's reclusive forest elephants and the herds that trundle across its savannas are as genetically distinct as leopards are from lions, and thus should be reclassified as separate species, geneticists say.

The new genetic evidence, together with recent studies of the animals' distinct skeletons, tusks and other features, makes a nearly ironclad case for splitting the two types, elephant experts said. Genetic differences showed that the two types of elephants diverged about 2.6 million years ago.

In the study, sets of genes were isolated from tissue samples obtained by shooting darts at nearly 200 elephants in a variety of forest and savanna herds around Africa. The geneticists looked for differences in the genes and intervening sections of DNA. The greater the differences, the further back in time two lineages separated. They also compared the two African types to Asian elephants, which are a different genus.

14

Shrieked the African tusker, near panic,
'Not enough to be made schizophrenic
    By the claims on our land!
    We're not even one band:
We are, science says, schizogenic.'

15

ELEPHANT FAMILIES OWE THEIR SUCCESS TO MATRIARCHS' AGE, SOCIAL SKILLS

AGE IS GOOD, IF YOU'RE AN ELEPHANT MATRIARCH

Researchers studying elephant families in Kenya's Amboseli National Park have shown for the first time that the older an elephant matriarch is, the more finely honed are her social skills, and that this knowledge is statistically tied to the reproductive success of her family's younger members.

In the study, families that had a matriarch 55 years old or older were 1000 times more likely to bunch together defensively only in response to calls from families they rarely encountered.

An elephant matriarch begs
To ask, 'Does this study have legs?
    Sure, any fool knows
    That experience shows.
Try teaching your gran to suck eggs!'

16

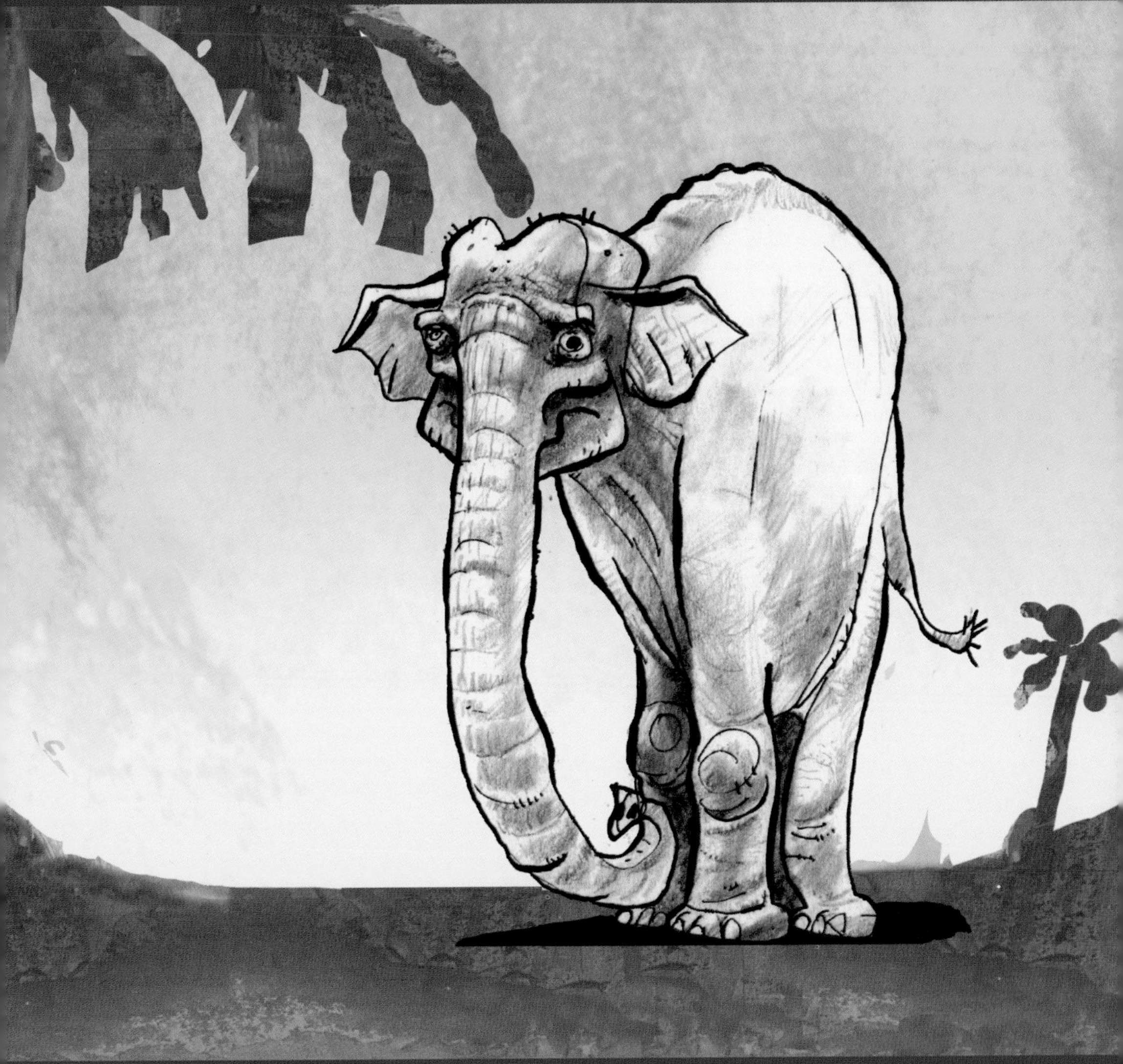

DUMBO NEEDS BIG EARS

If Dumbo the elephant were real he would have needed to flap his huge ears not just to fly but also to stop him overheating. So say two US scientists who became intrigued by the cartoon character while exploring how elephants cool themselves down by pumping blood through their ears. But his cooling system was so efficient that he would have died of hypothermia if he rested for too long.

The unusual study was carried out by biologists Polly Phillips and James Heath of the University of Illinois in Urbana-Champaign.

'It's all in the ears,' Dumbo said;
'And not just for lifting my head.
They won't let me die
Of the heat while I fly.
If it's cold when I rest, though, I'm dead!'

18

ELEPHANT FOSSIL FOUND IN KASHMIR

'This fossil is terribly old,'
Said the expert. 'It makes us all bold
To say Kashmir was hot;
Or, if it was not,
That this tusker just loved the cold.'

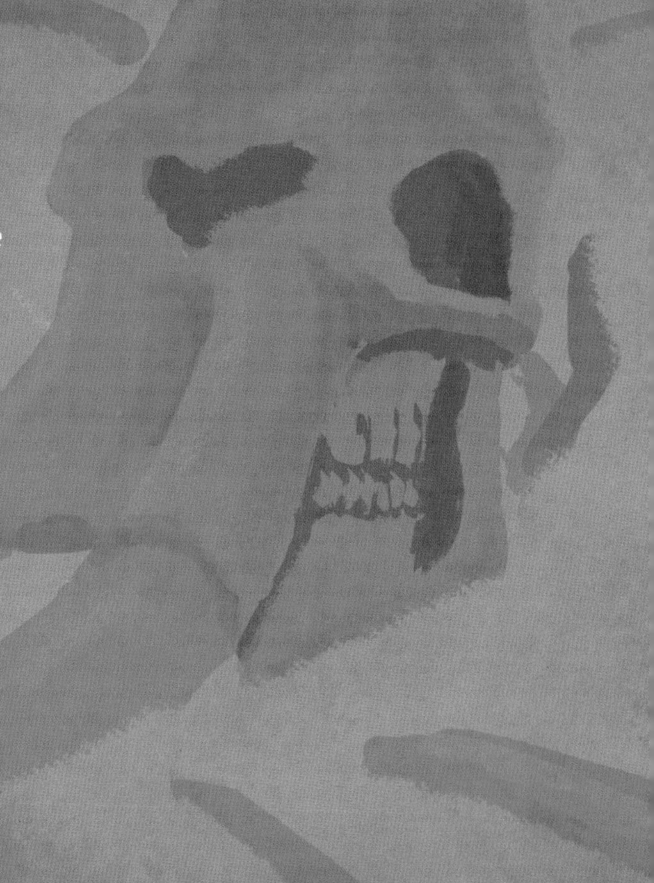

IT TOOK FOUR DAYS TO UNEARTH THE FOSSIL

Indian geologists say they have unearthed the 50,000-year-old fossil of an elephant in the state of Jammu and Kashmir. The geologists say this indicates that Kashmir, situated on the edge of the Himalayas, had a warm climate several thousand years ago.

The find consists of a skull measuring 5 feet by 4 feet (1.5 metres by 1.2 metres) with complete lower and upper jaws, a broken tusk and a vertebra.

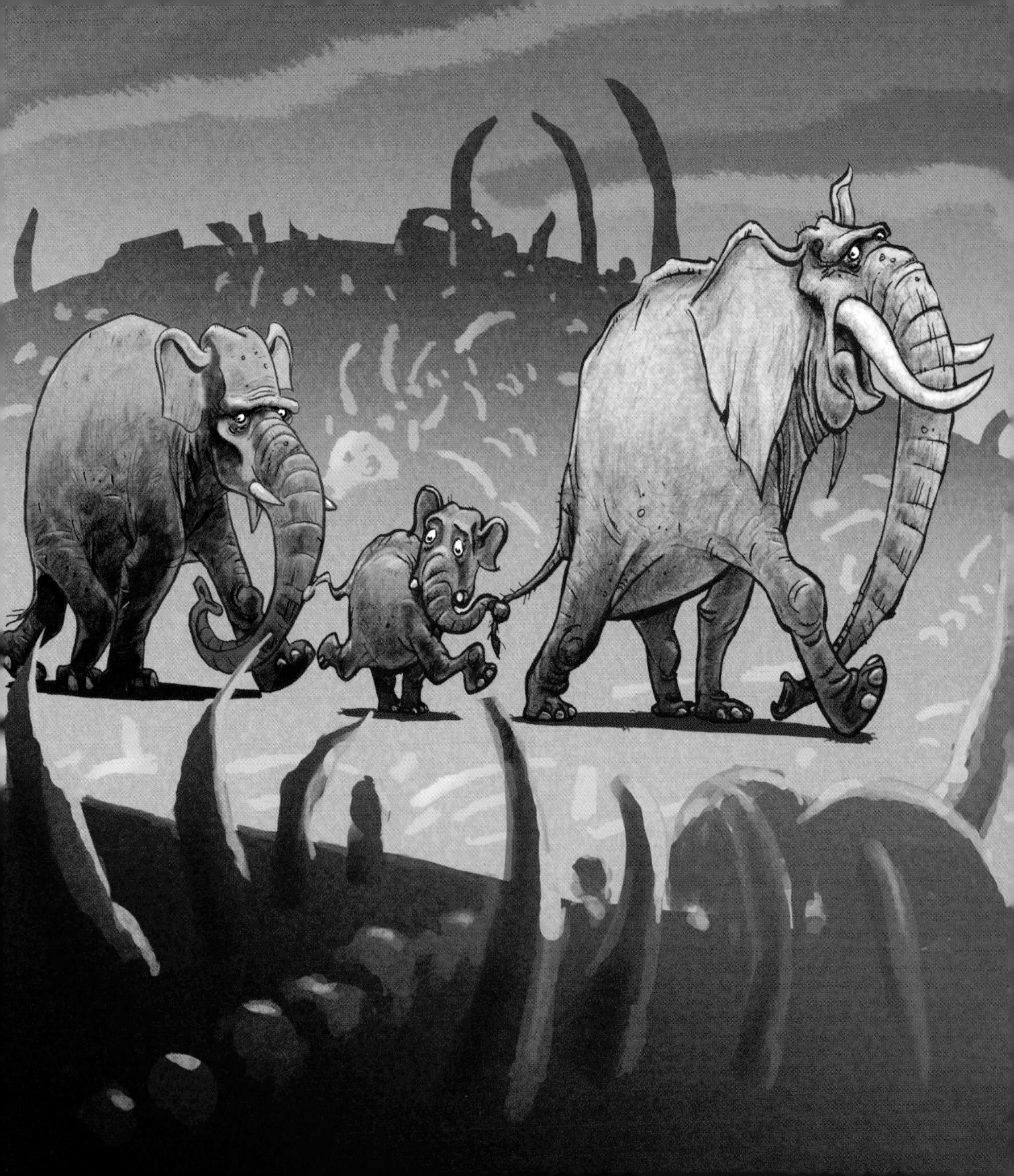

MAN AND OTHER ANIMALS

OUR FELLOW CREATURES HAVE FEELINGS — SO WE SHOULD GIVE THEM RIGHTS TOO

When it comes to the ultimate test of what distinguishes humans from the other creatures, scientists have long believed that mourning for the dead represents the real divide. Other animals have no sense of their mortality and are unable to comprehend the concept of their own death. However, elephants will often stand next to their dead kin for days, in silence, occasionally touching their bodies with their trunks. Kenyan biologist Joyce Poole, who has studied African elephants for 25 years, says that elephant behaviour towards their dead 'leaves me with little doubt that they experience deep emotion and have some understanding of death'.

Why do elephants seem to grow tense
At sites where their kind have passed hence?
Merely fear of the bones?
Or recall of last moans?
No! Refined metaphysical sense!

LOOKING FOR EARTH-SHAKING CLUES TO ELEPHANT COMMUNICATION

A research associate in the Stanford University School of Medicine, Caitlin O'Connell-Rodwell has come to one of Africa's premiere wildlife sanctuaries to explore the mysterious and complex world of elephant communication. She and her colleagues are part of a scientific revolution that began nearly two decades ago with the stunning revelation that elephants communicate over long distances using low-pitched vocalisations that are barely audible to humans.

In 1997, O'Connell-Rodwell took this discovery in a bold new direction by proposing that low-frequency calls also generate powerful vibrations in the ground — seismic signals that elephants can feel, and even interpret, via their sensitive trunks and feet.

GOOD VIBRATIONS

Elephants don't just feel the vibes, O'Connell-Rodwell says, they also transmit vibrational signals through the ground — long-distance seismic messages that could play a crucial role in their survival and reproductive success. 'Perhaps they're sending out signals to potential mates far away,' she says. 'Or maybe they can tell if a predator is in the vicinity by picking up seismic cues from a distressed herd.'

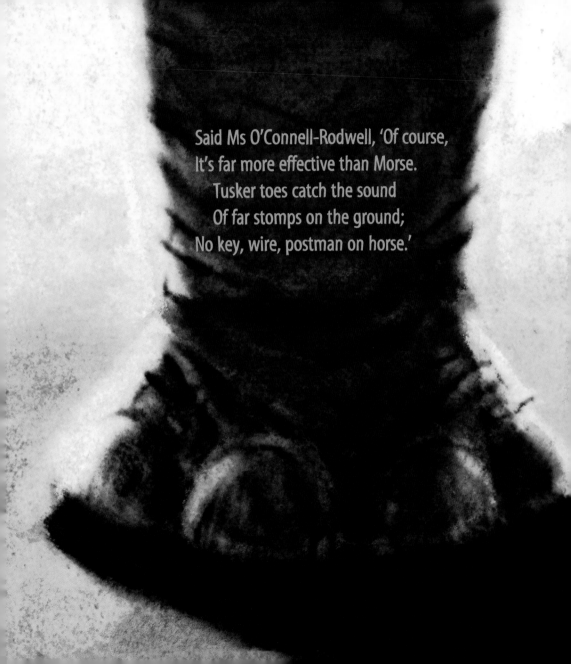

Said Ms O'Connell-Rodwell, 'Of course,
It's far more effective than Morse.
　　Tusker toes catch the sound
　　Of far stomps on the ground;
No key, wire, postman on horse.'

HOW TO GRAB AN ELEPHANT'S EAR

A ZOOLOGY STUDENT IS DEVELOPING A METHOD OF COMMUNICATING TO ELEPHANTS USING A DIDGERIDOO

James Gordon, a final-year student at Leeds University, believes that the low-frequency sounds from his version of the instrument can be used to warn the animals of danger. He came up with the idea after speaking to an Australian he was working with in Zimbabwe.

'The didgeridoo is able to create an infrasonic sound that elephants are able to detect from up to 2 kilometres away. From the distances I play, the human ear cannot hear the sounds I make. The whole project rests on being able to train elephants into recognising this sound and realising that it means they are approaching danger.'

Mr Gordon, 22, from London, has tested his didgeridoo communicator at Howletts Zoo in Kent, playing it to the elephants from a mile away. 'They reacted by pricking up their ears and observing around them. This shows that the sound was recognisable.'

Scientists have only recently discovered that elephants use low-frequency sound, below the level of human hearing, to communicate. Mr Gordon hopes to copy the exact sound they use. This month he is taking his didgeridoo to Blackpool Zoo to talk to the elephants there. Next year he hopes to return to Africa to try his ideas on wild elephants in the game parks.

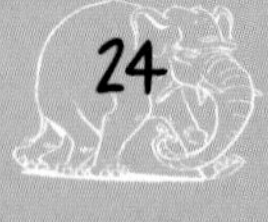

On the Tuskers' grapevine round the zoos:
'Have you heard the astonishing news?
Our mates in the wild
Will be soothed and made mild
By young James, with his didgeridoos!'

It might be effective in zoos,
Warning tuskers with didgeridoos.
But if it's so low,
Just how do we know
That that's what's conveying the news?

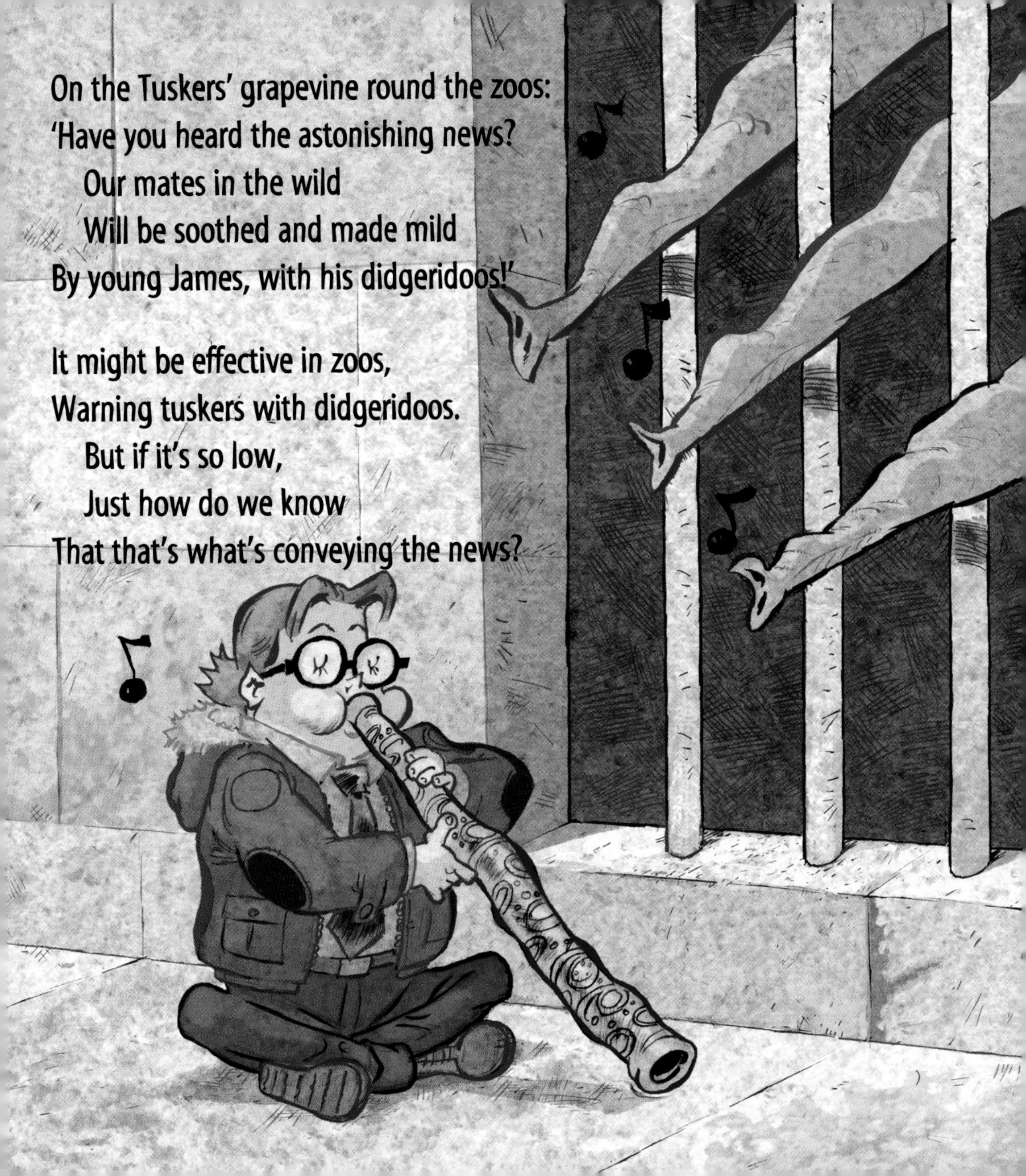

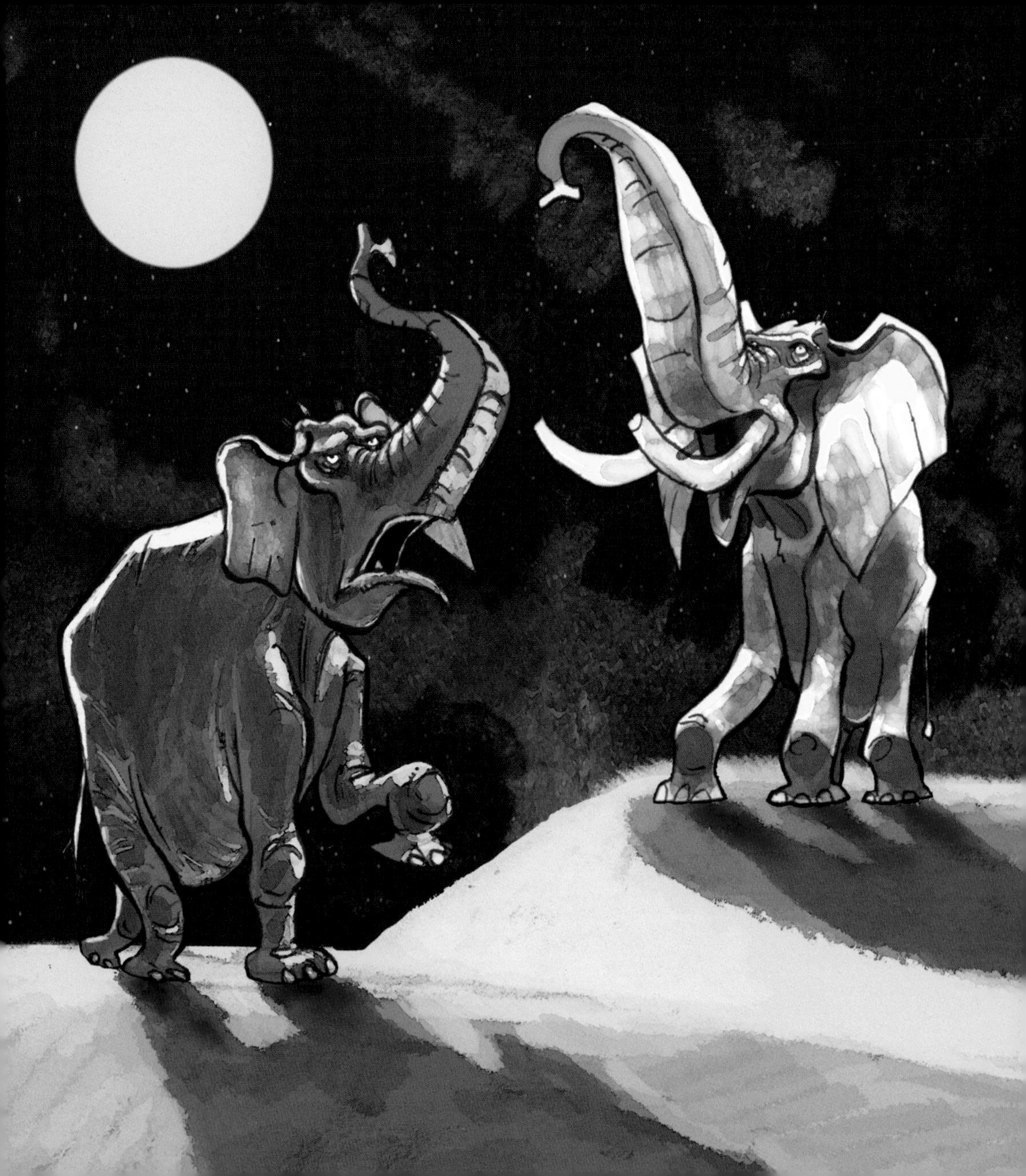

ELEPHANTS LIVE IN A COMPLEX SOCIETY BOUND TOGETHER BY DIFFERENT LAYERS OF COMMUNICATION

The majority of elephant sounds are made by adult females, juveniles and calves and very few by adult males. Of the 75 calls, adult females make 70 per cent, juvenile females and calves of both sexes 68 per cent, and infants of both sexes 33 per cent, while adult males make only 29 per cent. And of the 30 known low-frequency rumbles, adult females make six times as many as males.

'My Jumbo is one of the boys,'
Said Jessie; 'Completely lacks poise!
We females exchange
Sounds across the whole range;
But bulls make just one single noise.'

27

PROFESSOR HOPES TO CLONE MAMMOTH

A Northern Arizona University geologist aims to excavate and clone a woolly mammoth from DNA.The adult male mammoth, estimated to be about 40 years old when it became frozen, was found by a nine-year-old nomadic reindeer herder in 1997. Northern Arizona University geologist Larry Agenbroad and scientists from the Netherlands, France and Russia are removing the ice-encased animal from the Taimyr Peninsula in Siberia and airlifting it more than 200 miles to the city of Khatanga, where scientists will study the 11-foot-tall animal.

The cloning process involves putting DNA from the mammoth into an Asian elephant's egg that has been stripped of elephant genes. So even though an elephant would give birth, the baby would be a mammoth, not a hybrid.

Some scholars from North Arizona
Are hoping that one day they'll clone a
New Mammoth (like Dolly).
Says the host-tusker, 'Folly!
I'd rather conceive from a boner.'

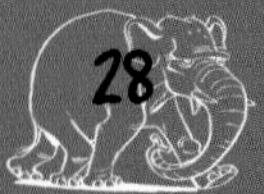

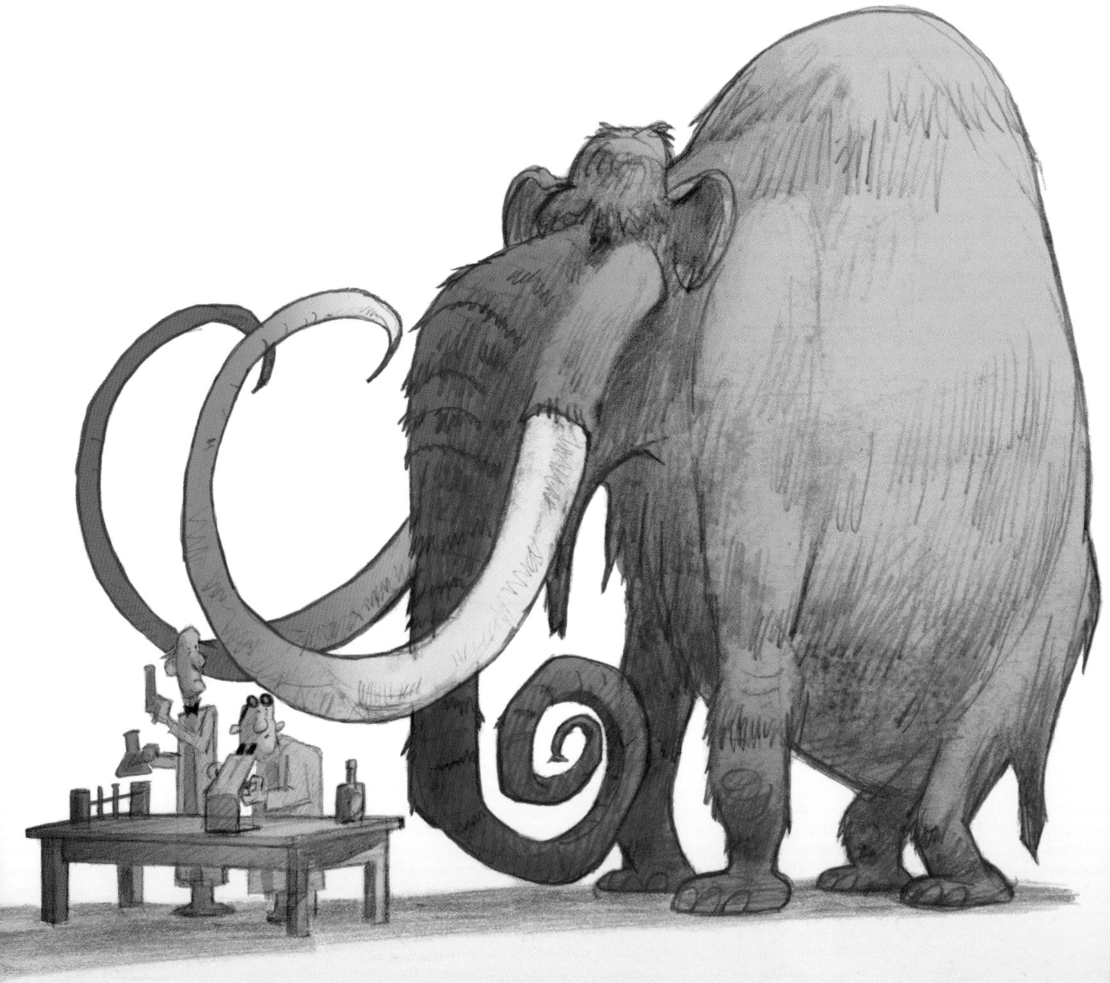

WOOLLY MAMMOTH RESURRECTION, 'JURASSIC PARK' PLANNED

A team of Japanese genetic scientists aims to bring woolly mammoths back to life and create a Jurassic Park-style refuge for resurrected species. The effort has garnered new attention as a frozen mammoth is drawing crowds at the 2005 World Exposition in Aichi, Japan. The team of scientists, which is not associated with the exhibit, wants to do more than just put a carcass on display. They plan to retrieve sperm from a mammoth frozen in tundra, use it to impregnate an elephant, and then raise the offspring in a safari park in the Siberian wild.

Many mammoth experts scoff at the idea, calling it scientifically impossible and even morally irresponsible. 'DNA preserved in ancient tissues is fragmented into thousands of tiny pieces nowhere near sufficiently preserved to drive the development of a baby mammoth,' said Adrian Lister, a paleontologist at University College London in England.

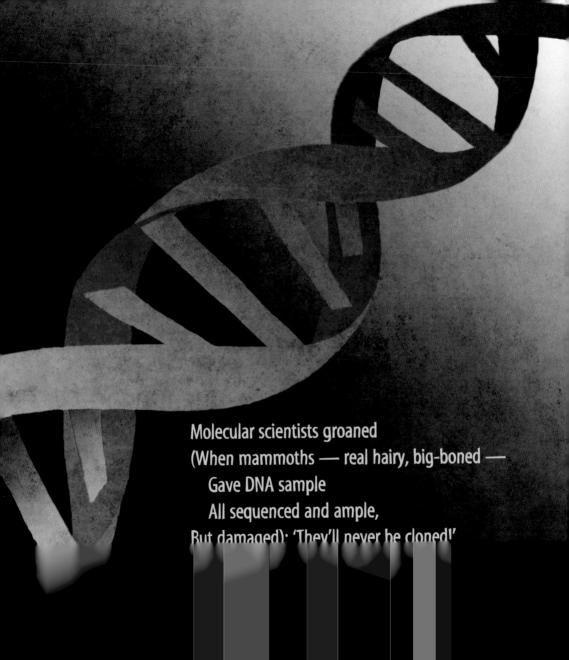

Molecular scientists groaned
(When mammoths — real hairy, big-boned —
　　Gave DNA sample
　　All sequenced and ample,
But damaged): 'They'll never be cloned!'

CHAPTER TWO:
ELEPHANTS IN LOVE

'When it comes to the matter of Cupid
We elephants surely aren't stupid.
   Affairs of the heart
   Make us warm from the start.
I'm just as romantic as you, kid.'

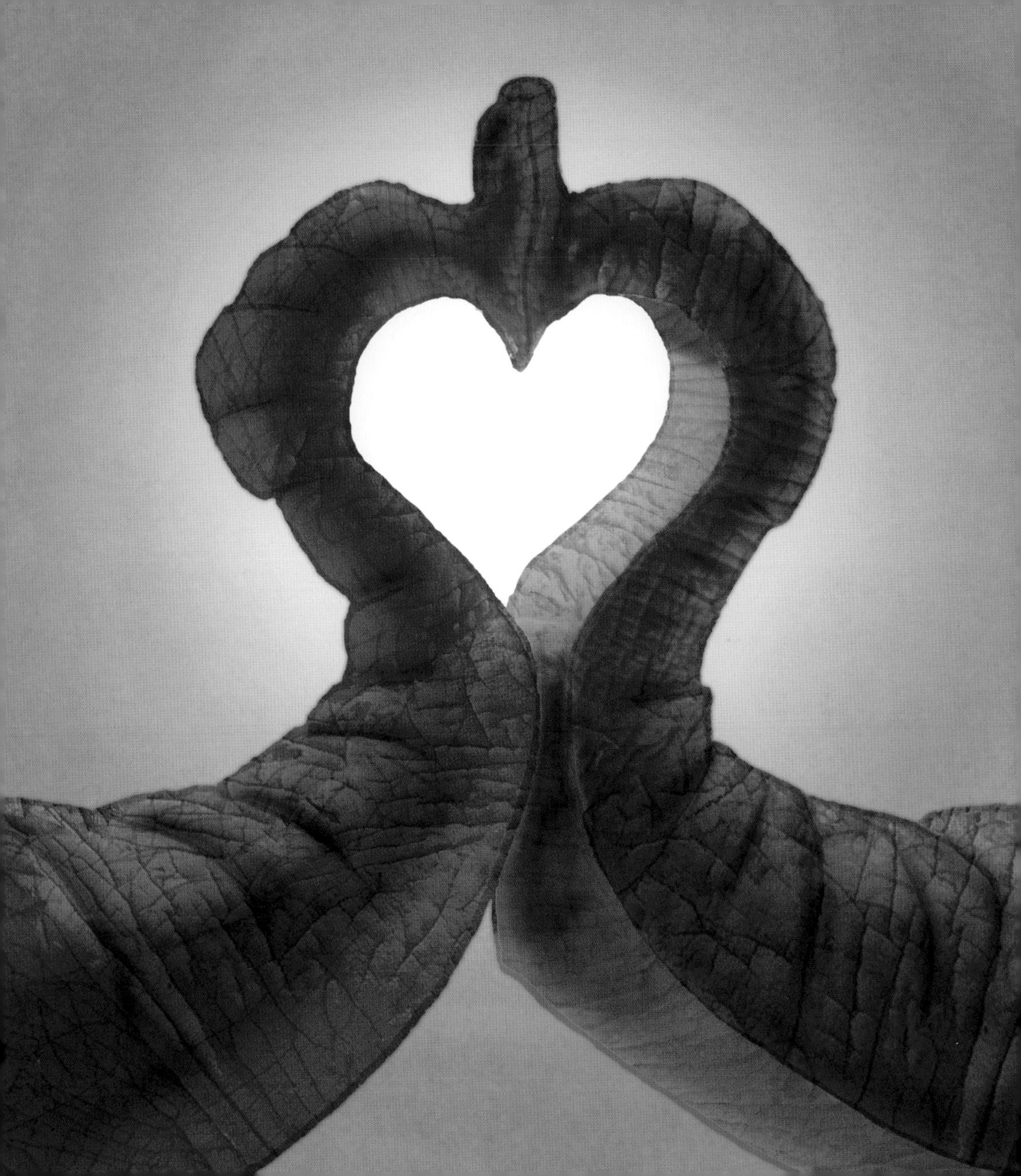

ZOO TOUTS SPECIAL ELEPHANT BIRTH

SPRINGFIELD, Missouri. (AP) — In an important milestone for an endangered species, an Asian elephant has given birth through artificial insemination.

Weighing in at 378 pounds, Haji was born on Sunday at Dickerson Park Zoo. It was the world's first birth through artificial insemination of an Asian elephant, which are estimated to number only 35,000 worldwide.

Because male elephants are very aggressive, they need special holding pens and can't be kept with females, making breeding options difficult. Scientists hope artificial insemination will alleviate some of the expense and difficulty of transporting males between breeding facilities.

Meanwhile, Haji and mom Moola are bonding nicely. After 674 days in his mother's womb, Haji was standing with assistance 20 minutes later and nursing three hours later. The elephants will remain off exhibit for several weeks. Zookeepers must now introduce Haji to the rest of the eight-elephant herd.

34

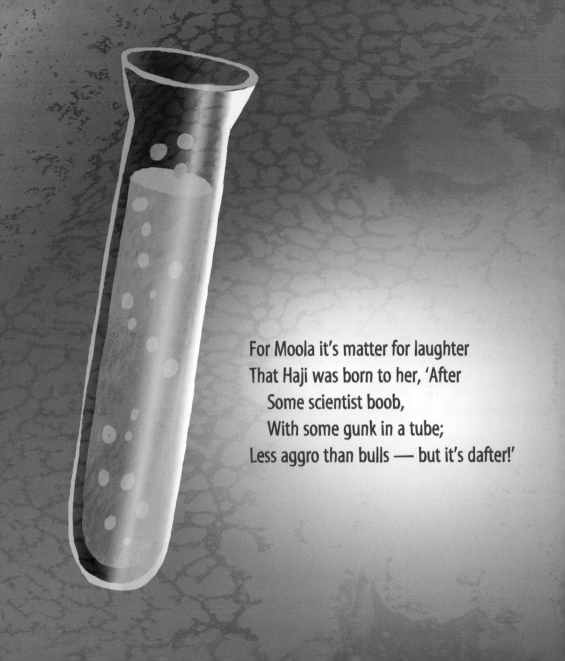

For Moola it's matter for laughter
That Haji was born to her, 'After
   Some scientist boob,
    With some gunk in a tube;
Less aggro than bulls — but it's dafter!'

ELEPHANT-SIZED FERTILITY TREATMENT

EXPERTS FROM GERMANY CARRIED OUT THE PROCEDURE

Tanya the African elephant, at Colchester Zoo, is almost three months pregnant. The insemination was carried out by experts from the Berlin Institute of Wildlife Medicine and Research. If the calf is born, it will be only the fifth elephant in the world to have been produced as a result of AI. The zoo decided to use artificial insemination after natural matings between Tanya and the zoo's bull elephant, Tembo, did not work.

Said Tanya to Tembo, 'Stop squirmin'
With shame. Yes, you did get your sperm in.'
 Old Tembo cried, 'Wait!
 When I've failed as a mate?'
Smirked she, 'You were helped by a German!'

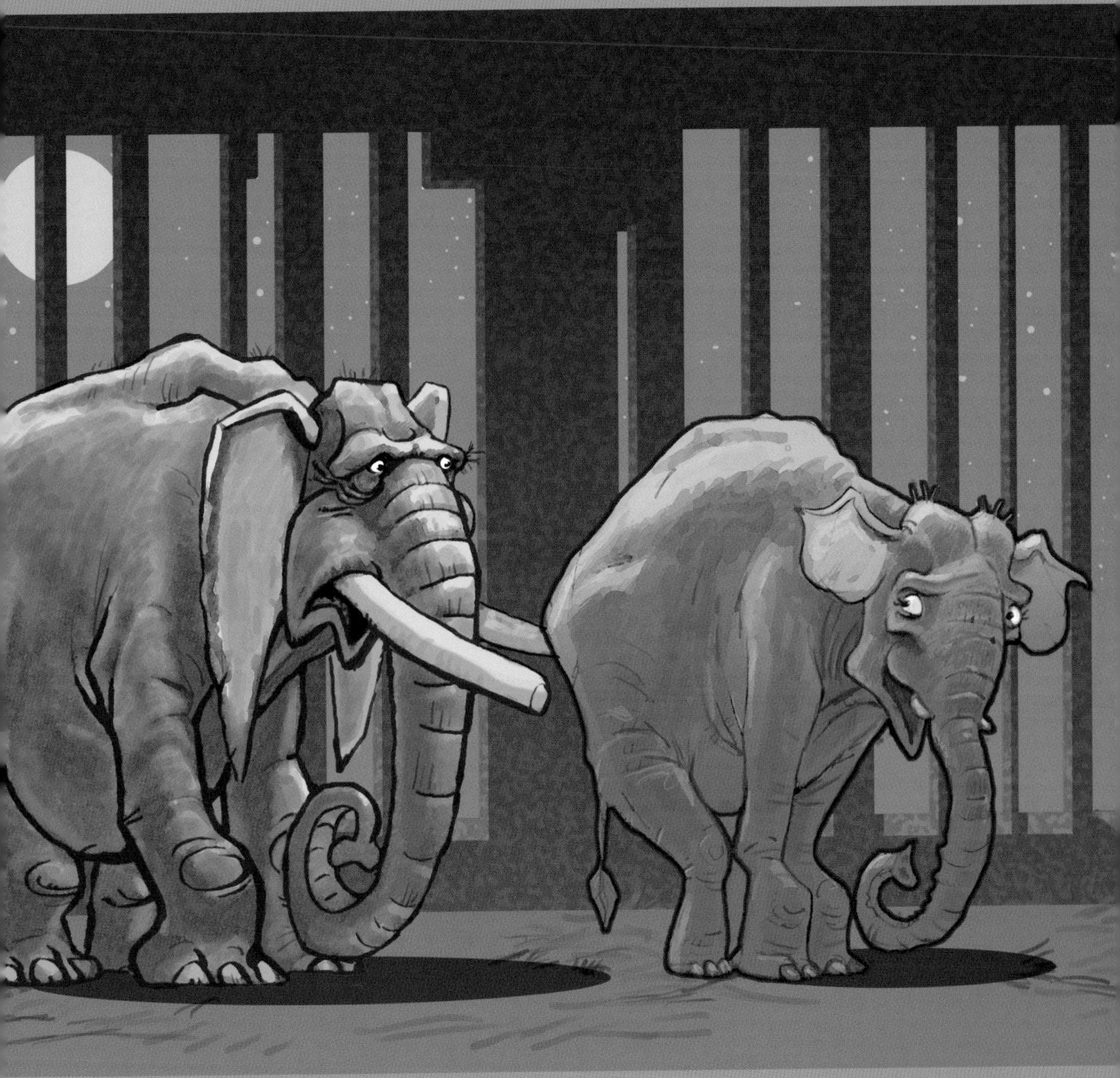

BREEDING ELEPHANTS CAN INVITE A TON OF TROUBLE

TOKYO — Micky, bilingual and thoughtful, shed 1100 pounds to win over Norame, the lone elephant stud in an animal kingdom north of Tokyo. But that romantic effort flopped, as have just about all efforts at breeding Asian elephants in Japan. Male elephants, it seems, have lost their sexual desire.

Japanese zoo keepers report all kinds of cases of unrequited love among elephants. As a result of these kinds of romantic difficulties, no one can remember when, if ever, an Asian elephant was born in Japan. As a result, Japanese zoos are going to considerable cost and distance to find elephants that like each other enough to produce calves. Norame was shipped in from Thailand for a one-year stay at a cost of more than $80,000.

Norame the elephant said,
'You ask why fertility's dead?
Yes, Micky's quite hale;
And there's zing in her tail.
It's me has the ache in the head!'

BULL ELEPHANTS FIRED
FOR FRISKY BEHAVIOUR

Bull elephants that for centuries have transported tourists to the hilltop Amber Fort in Rajasthan will lose their jobs in November because they can't stop thinking about sex. There are only nine males among the 97 elephants that carry tourists up the 1400-foot slope to the sixteenth-century fort near Jaipur, but it is the bulls who have been causing most of the commotion.

Last year, a female elephant carrying two Japanese women fell into a ditch along the slope after a male in rut bumped her from behind. After the accident the state tourism department wanted an immediate ban on male elephants carrying tourists. But the owners pleaded for more time to replace the bulls with females.

Oh come, Muse Erato. Come, sing!
In Rajasthan, Love is still king.
　　Bull tuskers, long tame,
　　Lost their jobs and risked shame:
On their minds there was only one thing.

39

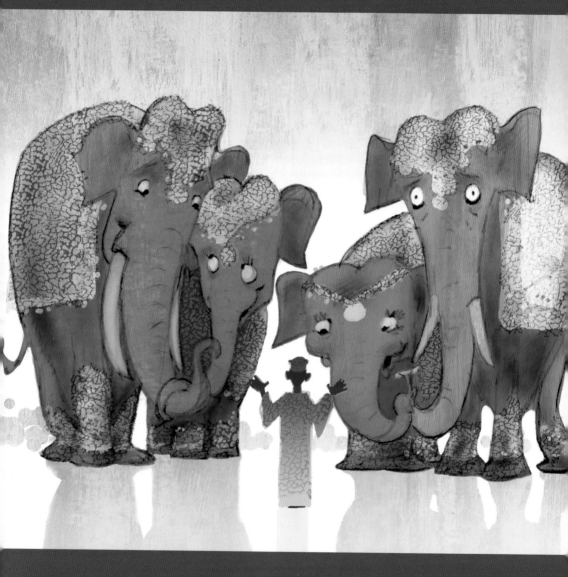

THAI ELEPHANTS TIE THE KNOT

Thailand's (and possibly the world's) largest honeymooners are relaxing after a Valentine's Day double wedding witnessed by hundreds of onlookers. Two elephant couples enjoyed a traditional Thai ceremony with all the trimmings before being whisked away to a post-nuptial retreat.

Afterwards, their mahouts (keepers) and local officials helped all four mark trunk prints on giant marriage certificates before posing in front of temple ruins for the official wedding photographs.

All four left in trucks for the Ayutthaya Elephant Shelter, about 70 kilometres (44 miles) north of Bangkok.

The most bizarre elephant lark
Since Noah unloaded his ark?
This time ('God be thankit!')
Right side of the blanket
Will veil their love-play after dark.

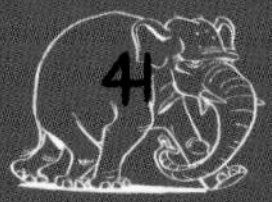

YOUNG BLOOD WITH A TASTE FOR TRUMPET

In the wild, Chang, a 17-year-old Asian bull elephant, would be too young and too junior to mate. But Chang has just impregnated two more females at Chester Zoo, bringing the number of pregnancies he is responsible for to eight, a record for a British zoo. His keepers say it is all because of his laid-back nature. Bull elephants can be difficult to handle but Chang has charm.

He is brilliant at detecting whether the females are in season, dipping his trunk into their urine and using the Jacobson's Organ at the top of his mouth to check for pheromones. In no time at all the females are flirting with him, rubbing their backsides into his face. Other bulls have failed at Chester but Chang, acquired from Copenhagen, is now so successful that he is attracting females from zoos all over the country.

Says Chang, 'They're amazed at my pace,
And the love that I spread round the place.
No mystery! You see,
It's the taste of the pee,
And the feel of their bums in my face.'

ELEPHANT DIES OF GRIEF

An elderly female elephant has died of grief at an Indian zoo after the death of a close friend.

Damini, who was 72, had befriended a younger pregnant elephant called Champakali at the Prince of Wales Zoo in Lucknow. But she starved herself to death in misery when Champakali died in childbirth.

Poor tusker, heart heavy and heaving,
Was mourning her sister-beast's leaving,
    In pain hardly borne.
    Morose and forlorn,
She starved herself; died from her grieving.

CHAPTER THREE:
ELEPHANTS IN CAPTIVITY

Growled a tusker, 'What raises my hackles
Is seeing my kind kept in shackles.
   In open-range zoos
   We just love to amuse.
Our reward is the public's fond cackles.'

44

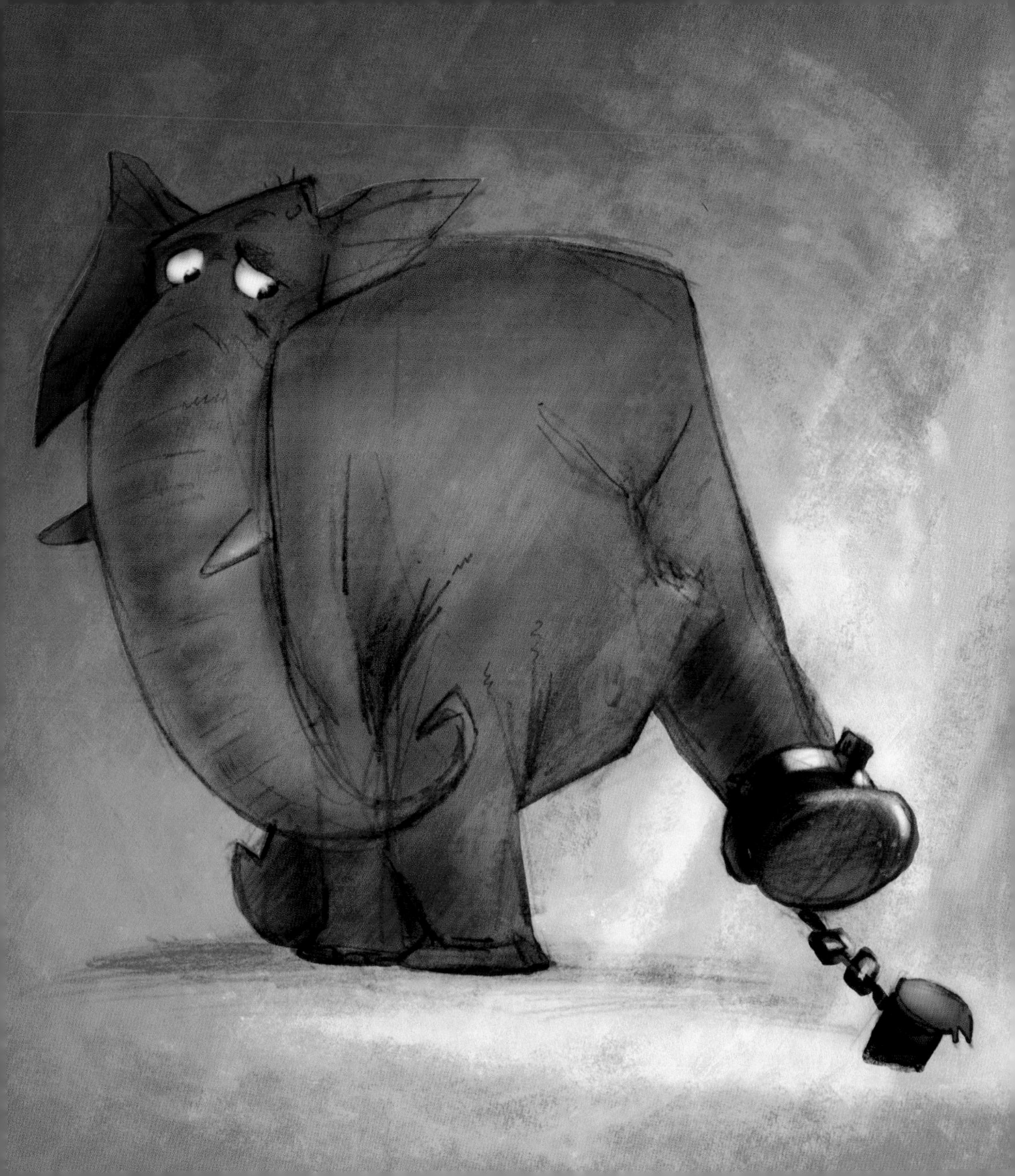

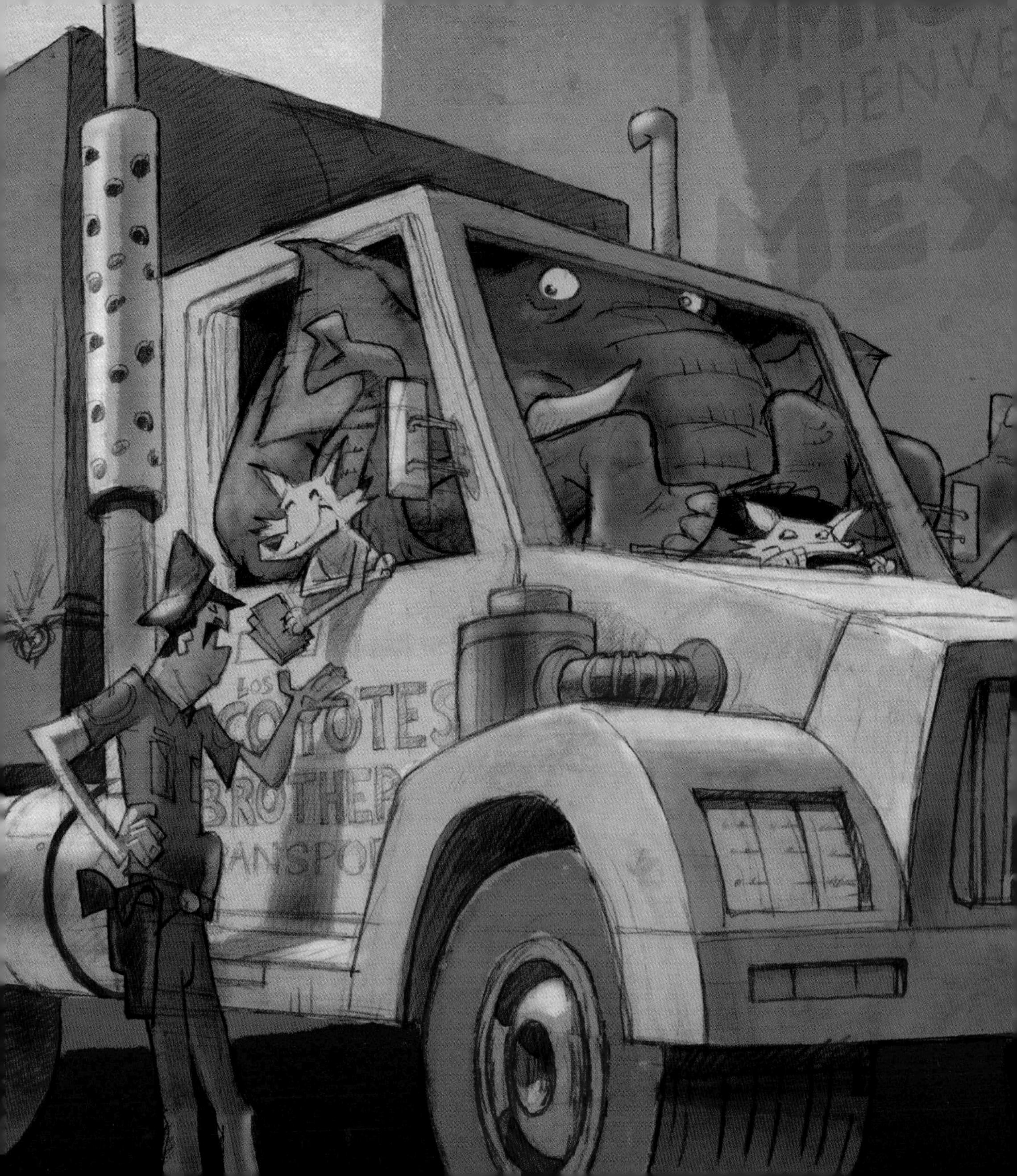
LOS

MAMMOTH BORDER SNEAK

A spokesman for the US Fish and Wildlife Service confirmed that a Texas elephant was smuggled into Mexico through a border checkpoint. He would not say when. He would not say how.

The owner of a Mexico City circus bought the Asian elephant from a Houston trainer and applied for the necessary permits from the United States and Mexico. But after a couple of months, he got tired of waiting. The owner then paid a 'coyote' $4500 to smuggle the 3-ton elephant south of the border in a five-wheel trailer pulled by a pick-up.

Mexican Customs agents passed the entourage through with a wave on April Fool's Day. But the punch line came months later, when Benny the Elephant — whose name was changed to Dumbo to keep his identity a secret — was discovered working in the Mexico City circus.

The Customs cry, 'Quite out of order!'
Senor Vazquez wails, 'Could I afford a
Month more to flow on?
The show had to go on!'
Dumbo trumpets *South of The Border*.

HEAVYWEIGHT TRAINER

When the city relinquished control of the zoo to the Toledo Zoological Society in 1982, Don RedFox was asked to fill in as elephant keeper until the zoo could get a permanent replacement. But then he was called upon to help select and train two young African elephants — and he hasn't looked back since.

The training of the elephants — and of RedFox — began in earnest with the arrival of Richard 'Army' McGuire. Recognised as one of the best in his field, Army had learned his trade by apprenticing himself to trainers in the circus — where his regimented ways earned him his nickname. As a circus trainer, Army connected RedFox to circus traditions.

RedFox's conversation comes back to the similarities of his relationship with his children and his relationship with the elephants. 'There's an emotional bond from me to them, and I'll say from them to me. When I've been away for a while and I go back to work, it's like I rose from the dead. There will be a lot of screaming and rumbling. You'll feel this subsonic communication. You can feel the vibration.'

48

'Zoo elephant-keeping well jibes
With bringing up kids,' Don prescribes.
  'Some circus traditions
  In army conditions;
And everyone rumbles good vibes.'

ZOO USED ELECTRIC RODS TO HANDLE ELEPHANTS

A British zoo yesterday admitted breaching European guidelines by allowing its keepers to carry electric prods when handling elephants.

Blackpool Zoo manager, Iain Valentine, insisted the cattle prods, or 'hotshots', were an integral part of the elephant management program. But the Captive Animals Preservation Society, which exposed their use by keepers of four Asian elephants, said it was appalled.

Old Valentine, down at the zoo,
Is causing his elephants rue.
With a 'hotshot' in hand,
He comes over all bland:
'This hurts me more than it hurts you.'

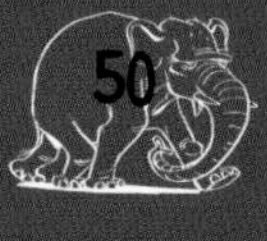

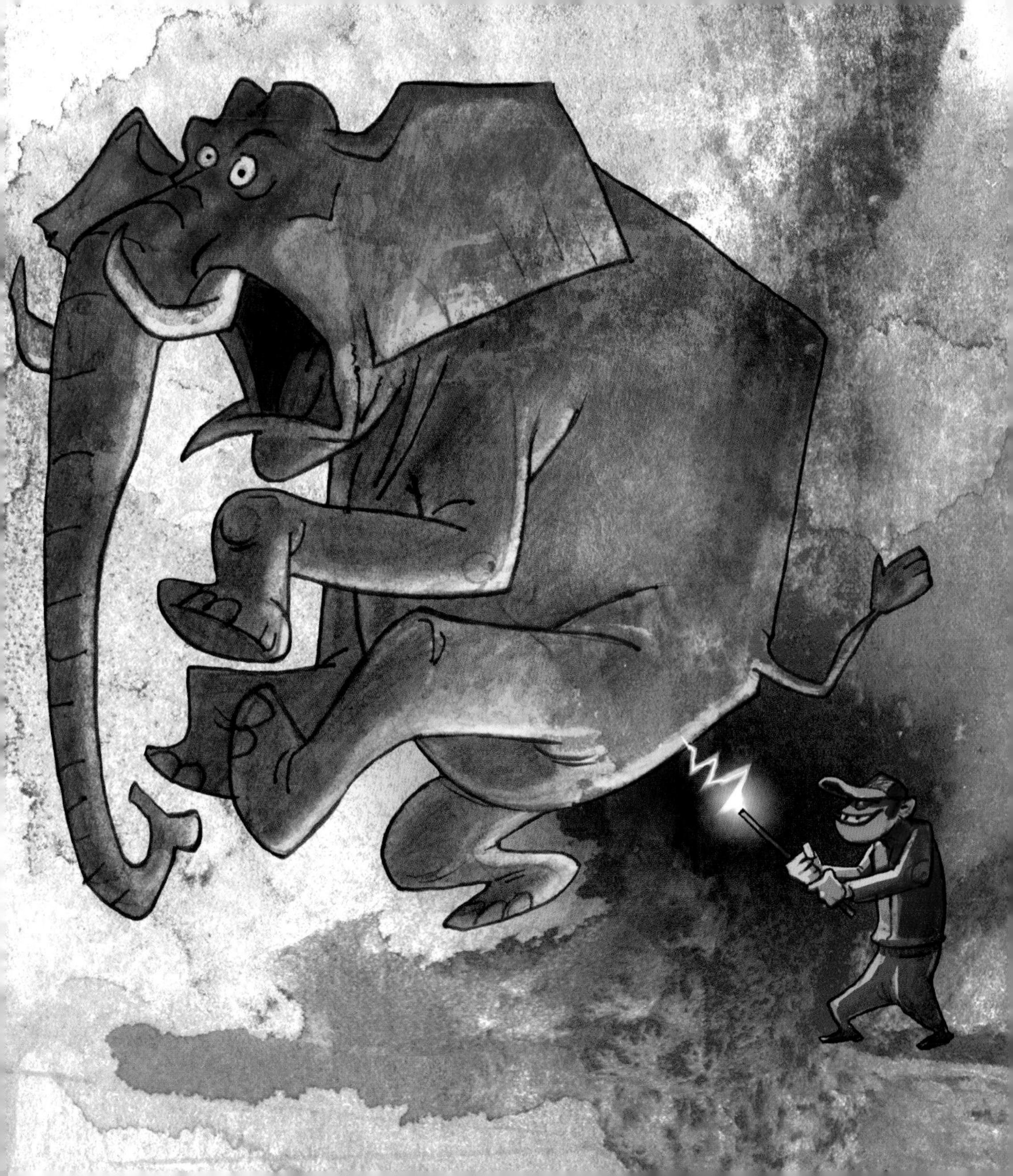

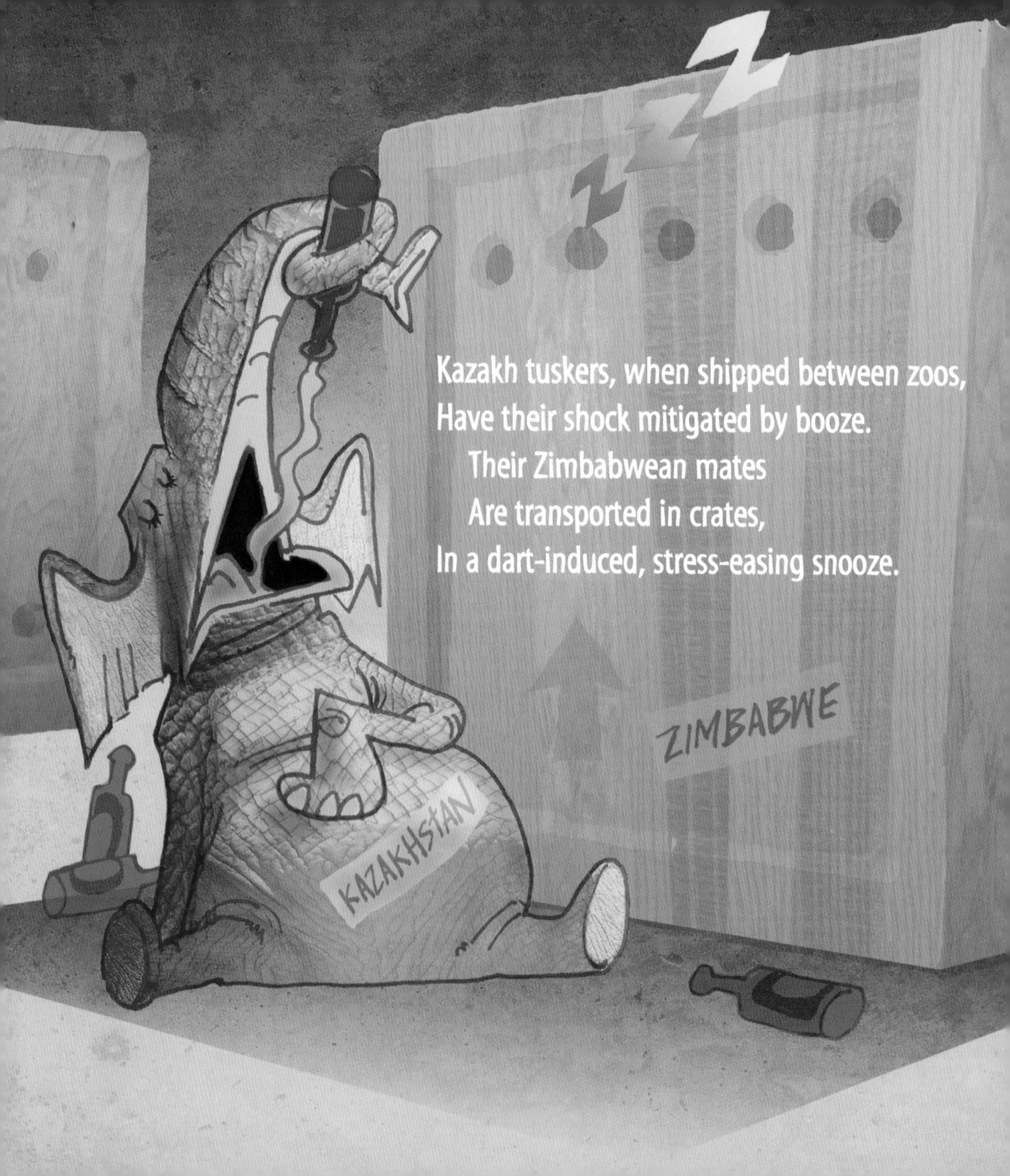
ZIMBABWE
KAZAKHSTAN

Kazakh tuskers, when shipped between zoos,
Have their shock mitigated by booze.
    Their Zimbabwean mates
    Are transported in crates,
In a dart-induced, stress-easing snooze.

KAZAKHS SOOTHE FRAUGHT ELEPHANT NERVES WITH VODKA

ALMATY (Reuters) — Four performing elephants were given 5-litre shots of vodka to relieve stress after a 20-day train journey to Kazakhstan's financial centre, Almaty.

The elephants, belonging to a Moscow-based circus, had to make a 4000-kilometre (2500 miles) journey across Siberia from Russia's easternmost port of Vladivostok.

The animals were held up for more than a day at the Russian–Kazakh border by Russian customs officials and again for nearly two days over the weekend in Almaty, because customs officials were not working.

In order to avoid a break-out, the four elephants were fed two crates of vodka, amounting to 5 litres each, and 360 kilograms (800 pounds) of vegetable snacks.

ELEPHANT MAN OF ZIMBABWE REFUSES TO FOLLOW THE HERD

A lot of heave-ho, shouting and doses of morphine and tranquillisers are the answer to the debate over what to do with too many elephants, according to Clem Coetsee, a Zimbabwean game expert.

Instead of mowing them down in bloody culls when overpopulation threatens to destroy their environment, Mr Coetsee knocks them out, loads them on to a pantechnicon and takes them wherever they are wanted.

Mr Coetsee recently moved two 25-year-old bulls that had wandered 100 miles from the Mavuradonha wildlife area in northern Zimbabwe to the maize fields of the Bindura valley 50 miles north of Harare. When he found them he leaned out of a helicopter with his dart gun and hit each beast with 8 milligrams of etorphine, an opiate 100 times as strong as morphine (a drop in your veins would kill you in 45 seconds) mixed with azaperone, a quick-acting tranquilliser to keep them placid when the anaesthetic wore off.

53

HUNGRY ELEPHANT CLIMBS TO SAFETY

HOW DO YOU GET A 51-YEAR-OLD, 5-TON PACHYDERM OUT OF A DITCH?

That was exactly the question French officials at the Lyon Zoo had to answer. After wandering away from his compound, Mako, the Asian elephant, lost his footing and slipped into a 6-foot ditch. A huge crane was brought in to raise the elephant. But that didn't work. Then, a ramp was built. But Mako doesn't like slopes.

Then they came up with an ingenious, albeit unconventional, solution — starve Mako out of the ditch. Sure enough, late Sunday night, the animal's appetite won out. After four days of starving, Mako made his way out of the ditch and is now back on his regular daily diet of 132 pounds of hay, beetroot, bran and protein.

Old Mako in France trumpets, 'Merde!
'Ow you say? Zat is surely ze word
To do full justice to
What zey're trying to do.
Send me starved up ze slope? 'Ow absurd!'

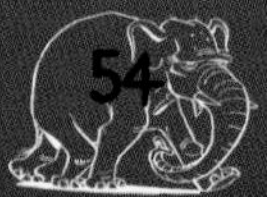

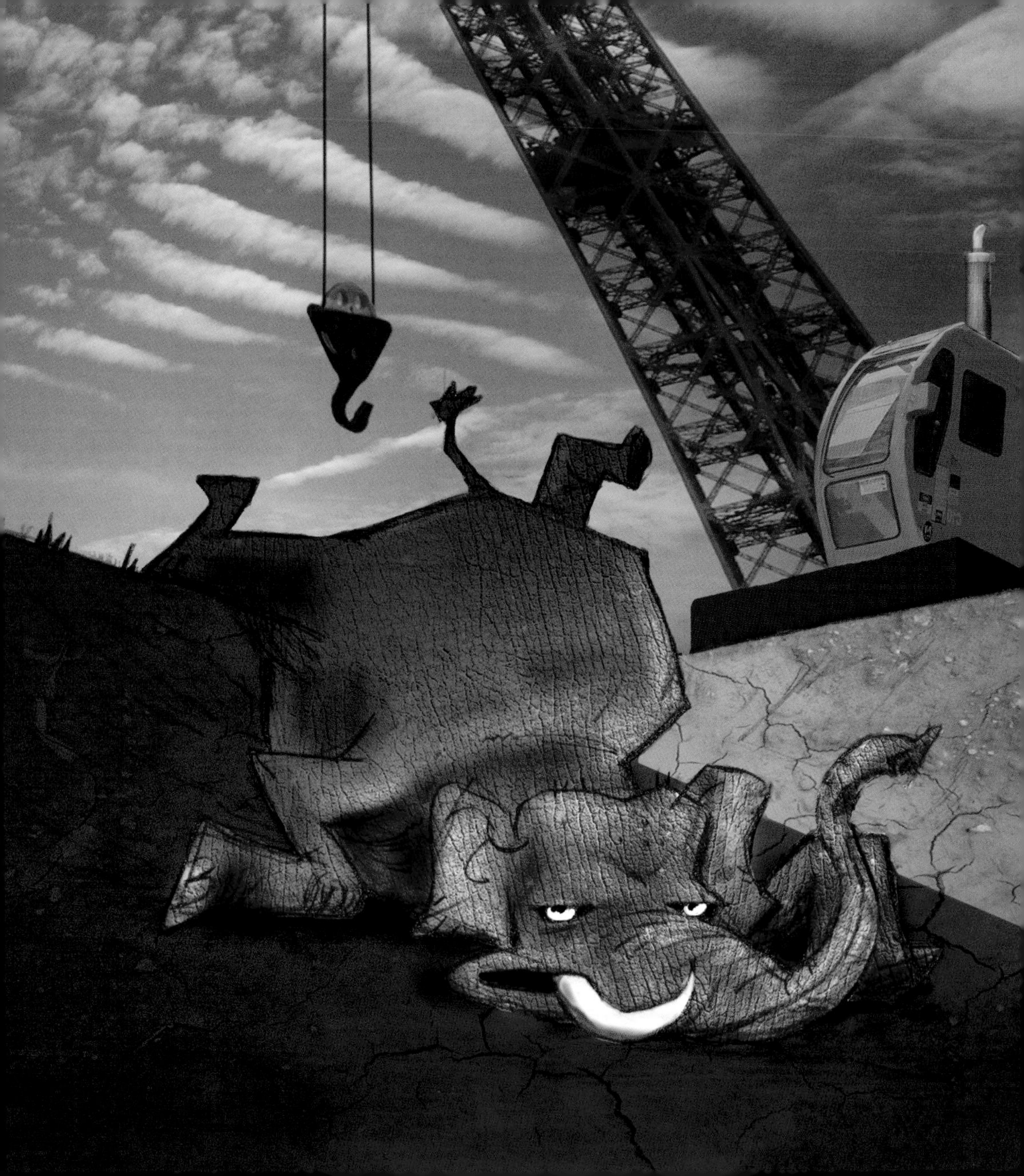

NAGGING QUESTIONS ON THE WISDOM OF ZOOS

The only elephants visible these days at the Lincoln Park Zoo's once-popular exhibit are the bronze mother and baby on a nearby drinking fountain. Wankie, the last of the three elephants, died last month after transport to Salt Lake City. Tatima and Peaches died in October and January. The deaths may be both natural and coincidental. But some animal-rights groups have used the deaths to rally support for their questioning of zoo practices, in particular the decision to display elephants, which they say need far more space than zoos can provide.

'These are the world's largest land mammals, they roam up to 30 miles a day in the wild, and zoos can't give them that kind of space,' says Debbie Leahy, director of captive animals and entertainment issues for People for the Ethical Treatment of Animals (PETA), which staged a protest at Lincoln Park last month.

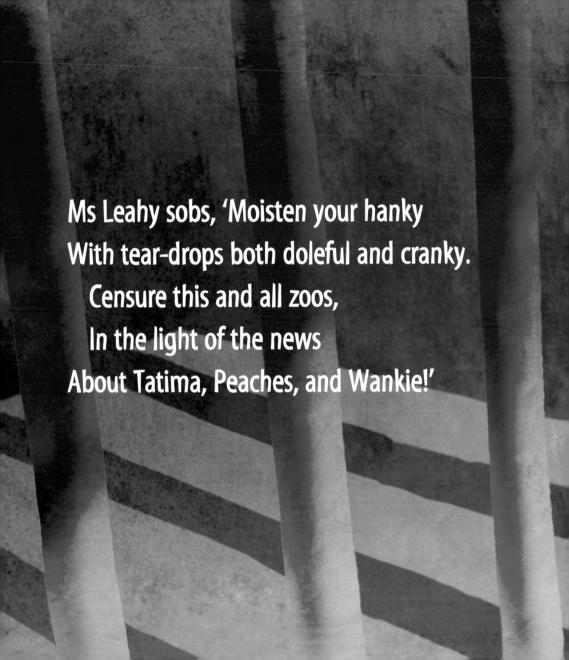

Ms Leahy sobs, 'Moisten your hanky
With tear-drops both doleful and cranky.
   Censure this and all zoos,
     In the light of the news
About Tatima, Peaches, and Wankie!'

CHAPTER FOUR:
ELEPHANTS ON THE JOB

It's not just a transient phase; he
Will toil till his eyes go all glazey.
This tusker's damp brow
Shows his worker's know-how,
As proof that he's never been lazy.

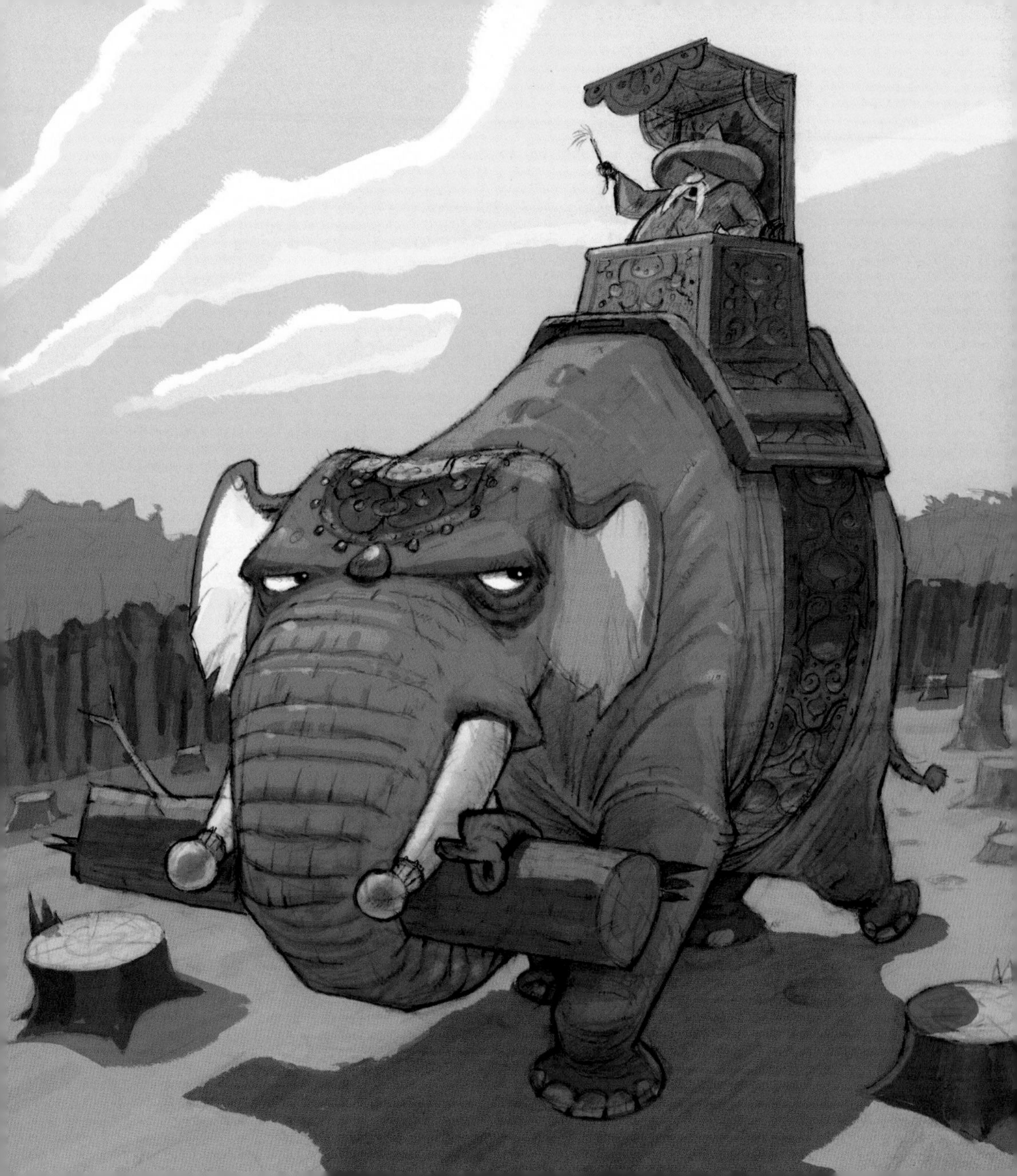

THAI NAVY TO RESCUE UNEMPLOYED ELEPHANTS

The Thailand navy has agreed to rescue three out-of-work elephants stranded on an island since the banning of elephant rides in the sea.

Their owner, Pongpayom Wassaputi, asked the navy to send a landing craft after he was unable to find a big enough raft to take them to the mainland, reports the *Bangkok Post*.

That Thai trio cries, ‘Hell! How dim!
Why must we bear bureaucrats’ whim?
Folks so liked to ride
Through the sea on our hide;
And we simply love a cool swim.’

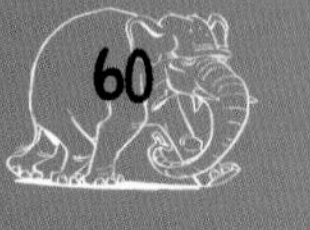

MINISTER WEIGHS ELEPHANT-IMPORT REQUEST

The current upgrading of the Taronga Zoo in Sydney and the Western Plains Zoo at Dubbo includes plans to re-introduce elephant-rides on some of the four young Asian elephants due to arrive in Sydney. Taronga's present tusker residents, Ranee and Burma, are to be removed to Dubbo. Animal-rights activists have reacted angrily to the planned elephant-rides. The decision on whether to allow the zoo to import Asian elephants for breeding purposes rests with the Federal Environment Minister.

'Those crazy PC types again!'
Said Ranee. 'They give us a pain!
To give kiddies a ride
Is both fun and our pride,
In Sydney and out on the plain.'

61

CRUELTY TO BEREFT CIRCUS ELEPHANT?

AUSTRALIA — The New South Wales Exhibited Animals Act requires that performing elephants must always be able to see and touch other elephants. The New South Wales Department of Agriculture and Stardust Circus have been charged with cruelty under the Act towards a 44-year-old elephant, Arna, which has had no contact with elephants since the death of her female companion, Bambi, in 1996.

MAGISTRATE REJECTS ELEPHANT-CRUELTY CHARGE

A magistrate has ruled that Arna had not been treated cruelly by being kept alone in a circus since the death of her fellow elephant, Bambi. Costs were awarded against Animal Liberation New South Wales.

Sighed Arna, 'They don't know the score.
Dear Bambi was such an old bore!
   For years upon years
   She just irked me to tears.
I like my own company more!'

'Those Animal Libbers, you know,'
Mused Arna. 'Officious! Although
   Poor Bambi's gone West,
   It's all for the best;
I'm elephant star of the show!'

62

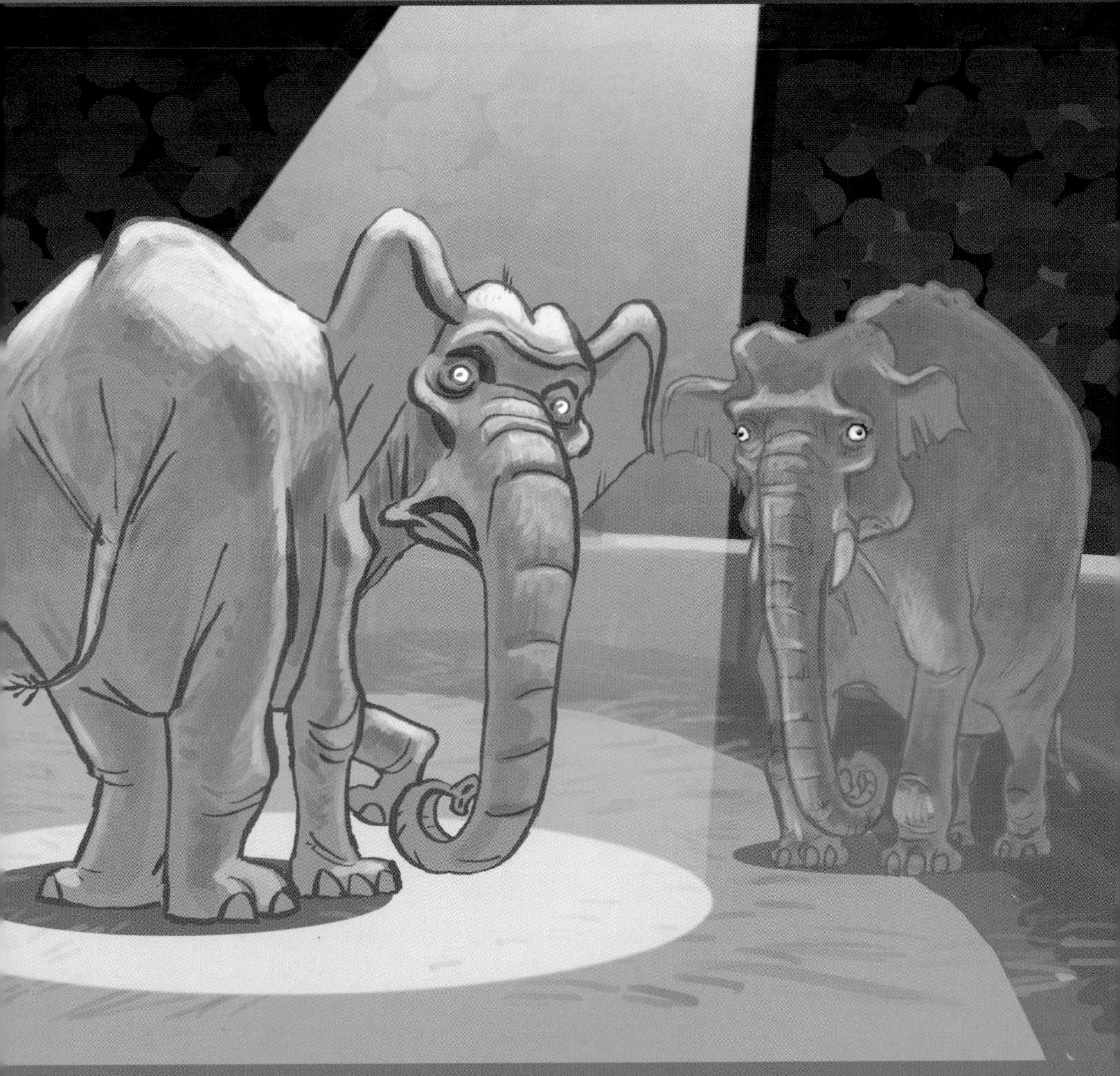

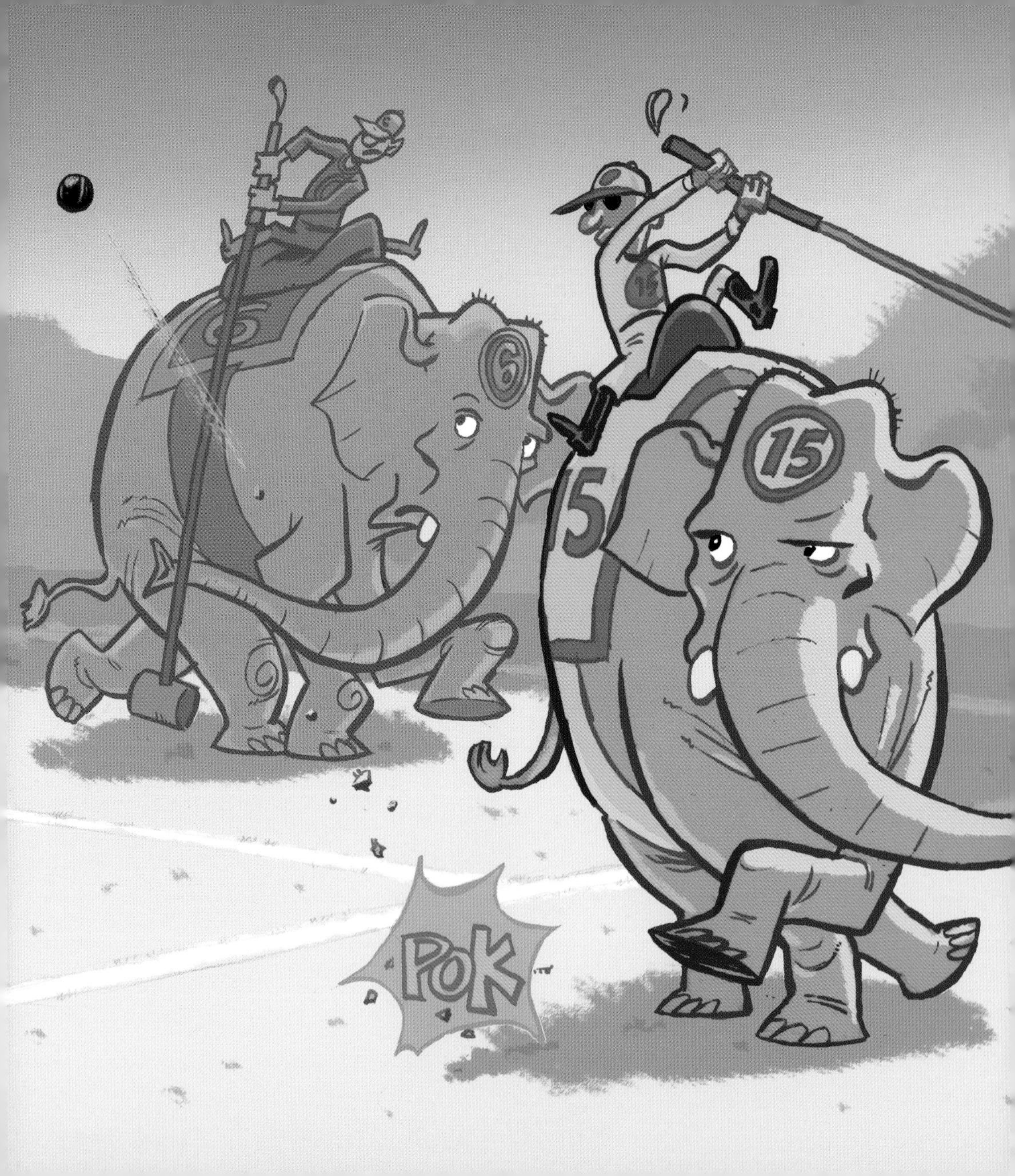
POK

SPORT OF KINGS

STAGE SET FOR FIRST-EVER ELEPHANT POLO TOURNAMENT IN HUA HIN

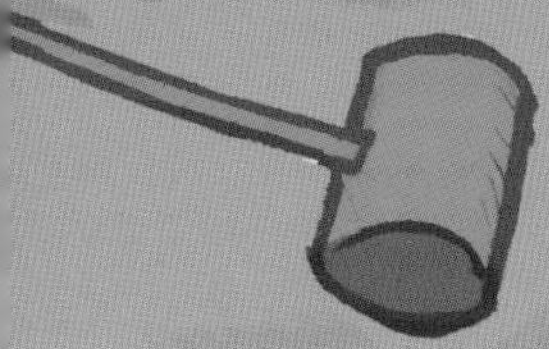

Anantara Resort & Spa, Hua Hin, together with the Elephant Conservation Centre of Thailand is proud to announce the first-ever Elephant Polo Tournament in Thailand. Teams confirmed to play are Nepal, Sri Lanka, Australia, Singapore and two teams from Thailand.

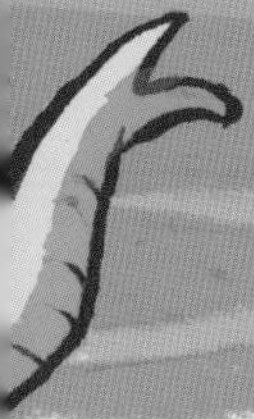

Gushed the Sri Lankan tusker, 'Let's chukka!
The polo set's really so pukka!
So very top-hole! Oh,
And as for the polo —
We play to conserve, not for tucker!'

POLICE SEIZE ELEPHANTS FROM CIRCUS

MONTEFIORE DELL'ASO, Italy (Reuters) — Police seized two Indian elephants from a circus in provincial Italy and transported them to Rome on Thursday, saying they had been imported illegally.

Forestry police used two cranes to hoist the elephants, who weigh around 4 tonnes each, into a container before driving them to a sanctuary for old and sick animals.

Magistrates have opened an inquiry into how the elephants arrived in Italy — a country which struggles to stem the flow of illegal immigrants but usually just has to deal with humans.

Forestry police say the circus owner bought the elephants in the Middle East and registered them on an out-of-date licence granted for two elephants which had long since died. Environment Minister Willer Bordon said when asked about the case, 'Acts with tigers, elephants and other animals are always the most popular, especially with children, but maybe it would be better to allow these poor beasts to live in their natural environment.'

Us elephants, how Ities jerk us
Around! And arrest us, and irk us.
They'd rather us home.
Imagine! In Rome,
The joint that invented the circus!

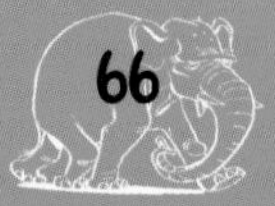

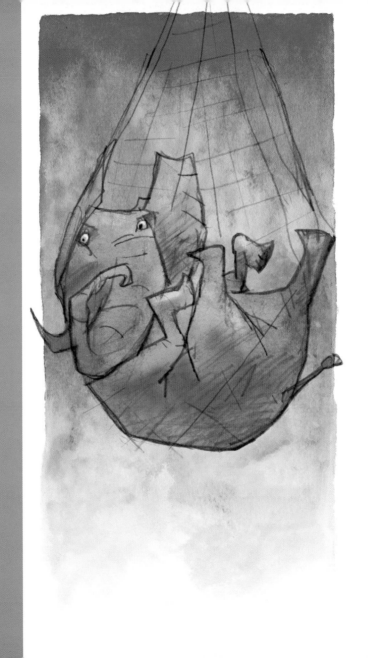

MICROCHIPS TO TRACK ERRANT ELEPHANTS

BANGKOK (Reuters) — Elephants brought illegally into Bangkok's city limits will get microchip implants so authorities can track their movements. Dozens of elephants wander the streets of Bangkok in violation of city regulations with their mahouts, or keepers, making a fast buck by charging people to feed or take pictures with the beasts.

Authorities were acting after animal lovers raised an outcry over exploitation of the animals and complaints from motorists. Offending mahouts will have their elephants rounded up, implanted with the chip, and trucked out of the city to their home provinces. Authorities will then track the elephants to make sure they do not re-enter city limits.

Bangkok elephants moan to each other,
'Bureaucracy's really a mother!
Chase bucks in the city;
Admin throws a shitty,
And it's microchips; watched by Big Brother!'

68

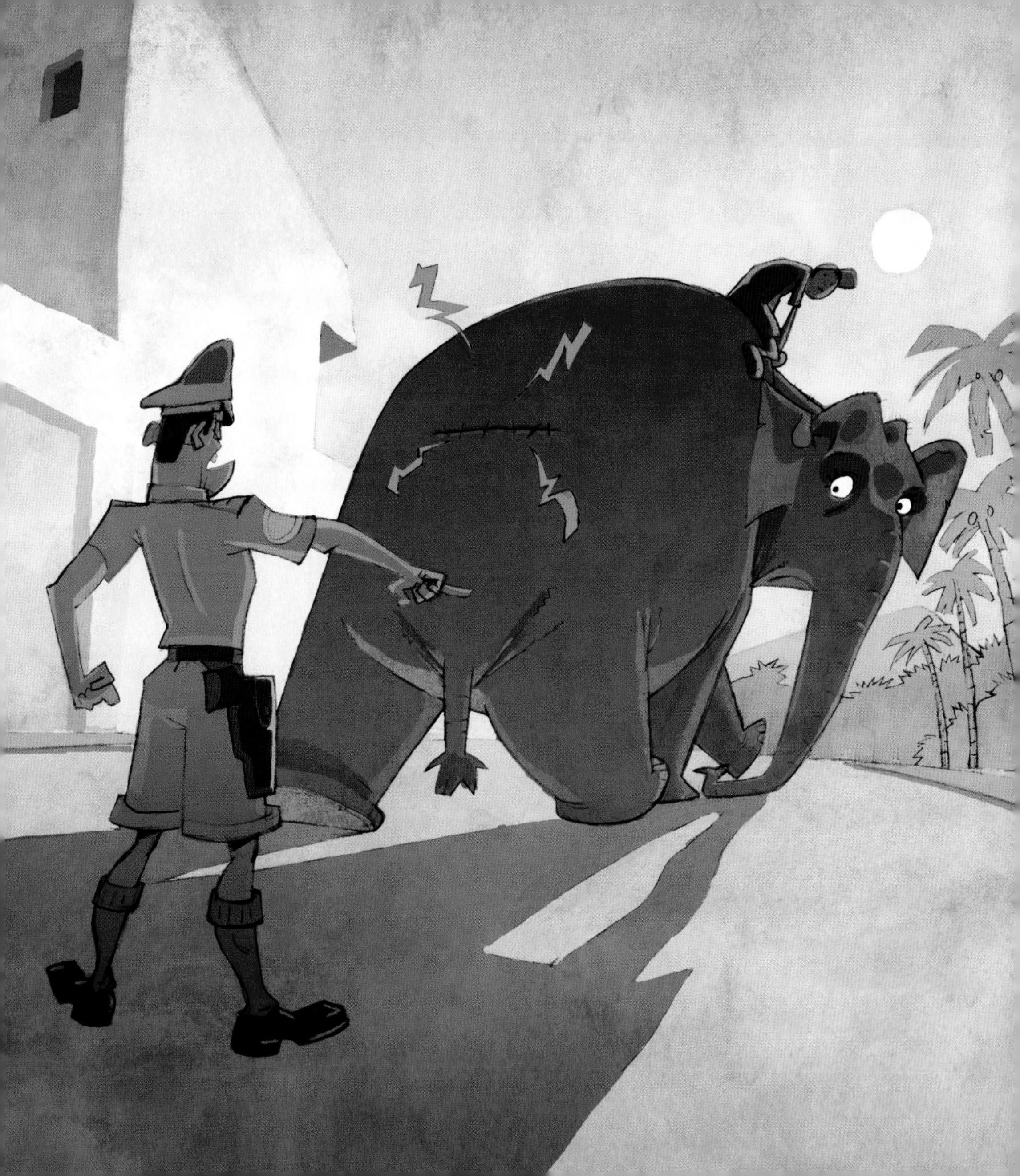

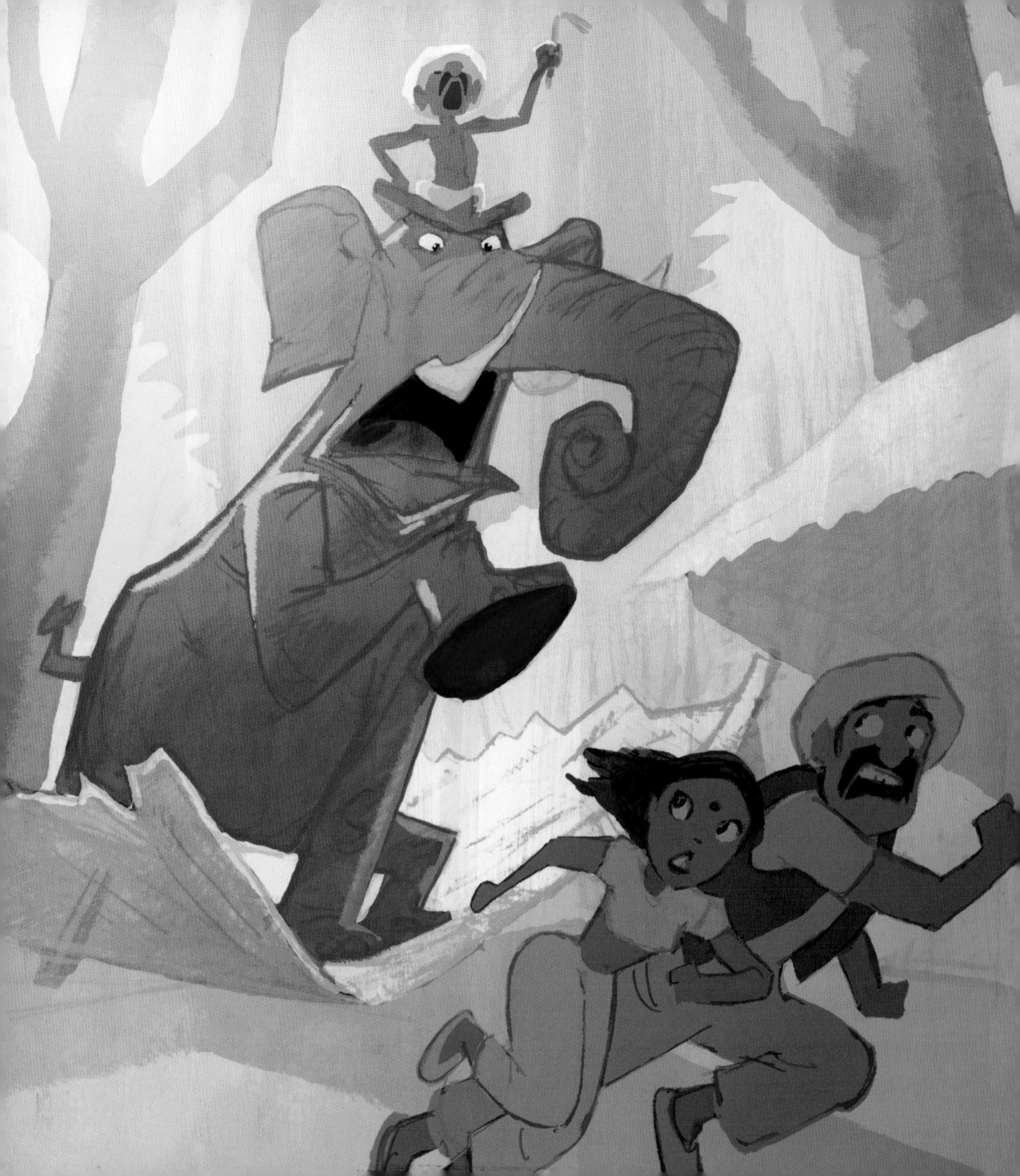

ELEPHANTS EVICT SQUATTERS

A tusker in Assam snarled, 'Squatters
Making homes in our forest, the rotters!
    Please pardon my grousing;
    It's not just thatch housing
I'd like to stomp under my trotters!'

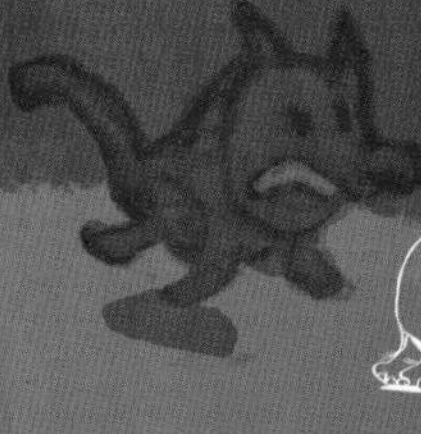

Authorities in northeastern India are using elephants as bulldozers to demolish illegally built houses. Five elephants have been drafted into service to break up about 1000, two-room, thatched houses in a protected forest area around Guwahati, the main city in the remote tea- and oil-rich state of Assam.

First the elephants, guided by their mahout, or trainer, remove the roofs with their trunks. Then they push over the bamboo walls and crush them with their feet. The pachyderms are being employed to clear 220 hectares (540 acres) occupied by 4000 people following a court order to restore the hilly, lush land to its protected status.

CHAPTER FIVE:
ELEPHANTS ON THE RAMPAGE

All tuskers have motion majestic;
Their baggy-pants march is their best trick.
　　But, should danger gape,
　　Their ways of escape
Can frighten, because they've egressed quick.

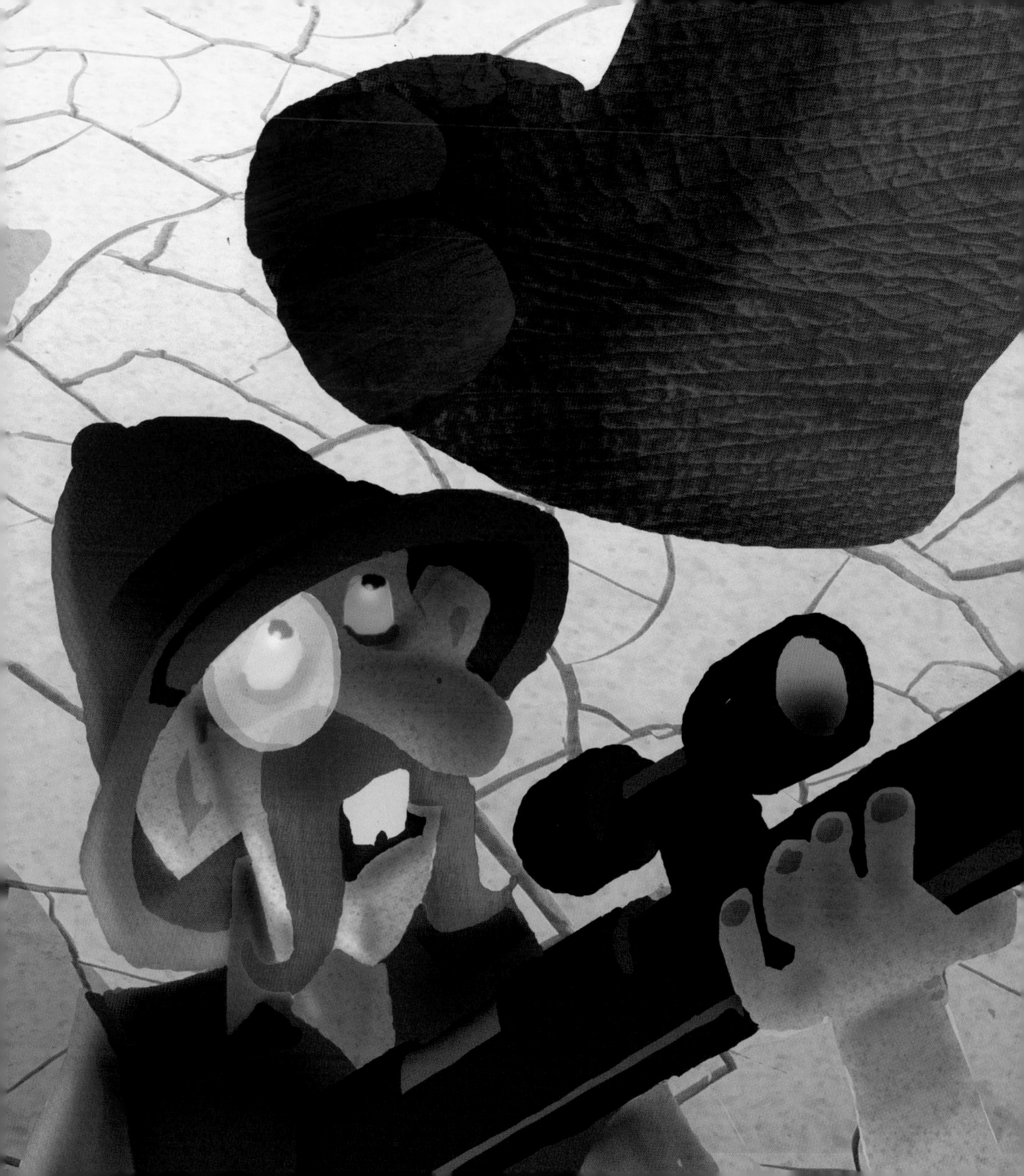

RAMPAGING ELEPHANTS ADD TO ORISSA'S WOES

INDIA — To Orissa's disasters of wind, tidal waves, floods, hunger, thirst and disease, a new terror has been added: rampaging hungry elephants.

Until 18 days ago, Chandaka Elephant Sanctuary's 70-kilometre-long fence penned the herds of wild elephant; groves of bamboo provided plentiful food. But when the 250 kilometre per hour winds struck on 29 October, practically every bamboo was uprooted and in several places the perimeter fence was destroyed.

Now the elephants are hungry and from ten villages around the sanctuary's periphery reports are coming in of herds searching for food and terrifying inhabitants.

The state's administration, not a byword for efficiency at the best of times, appears to have crumbled under the disaster's impact. A few days after the cyclone, the state's Chief Secretary, S. B. Mishra, the top bureaucrat responsible for implementation of policy, took leave and flew to the United States, where his daughter had become ill. Several other officials, including district collectors, followed his example and deserted their posts.

74

So, are Orissa's elephants shirty?
Well why not? When the weather turned dirty
    And trashed their bamboo,
    Public servants shot through,
Making aid-distribution too squirty.

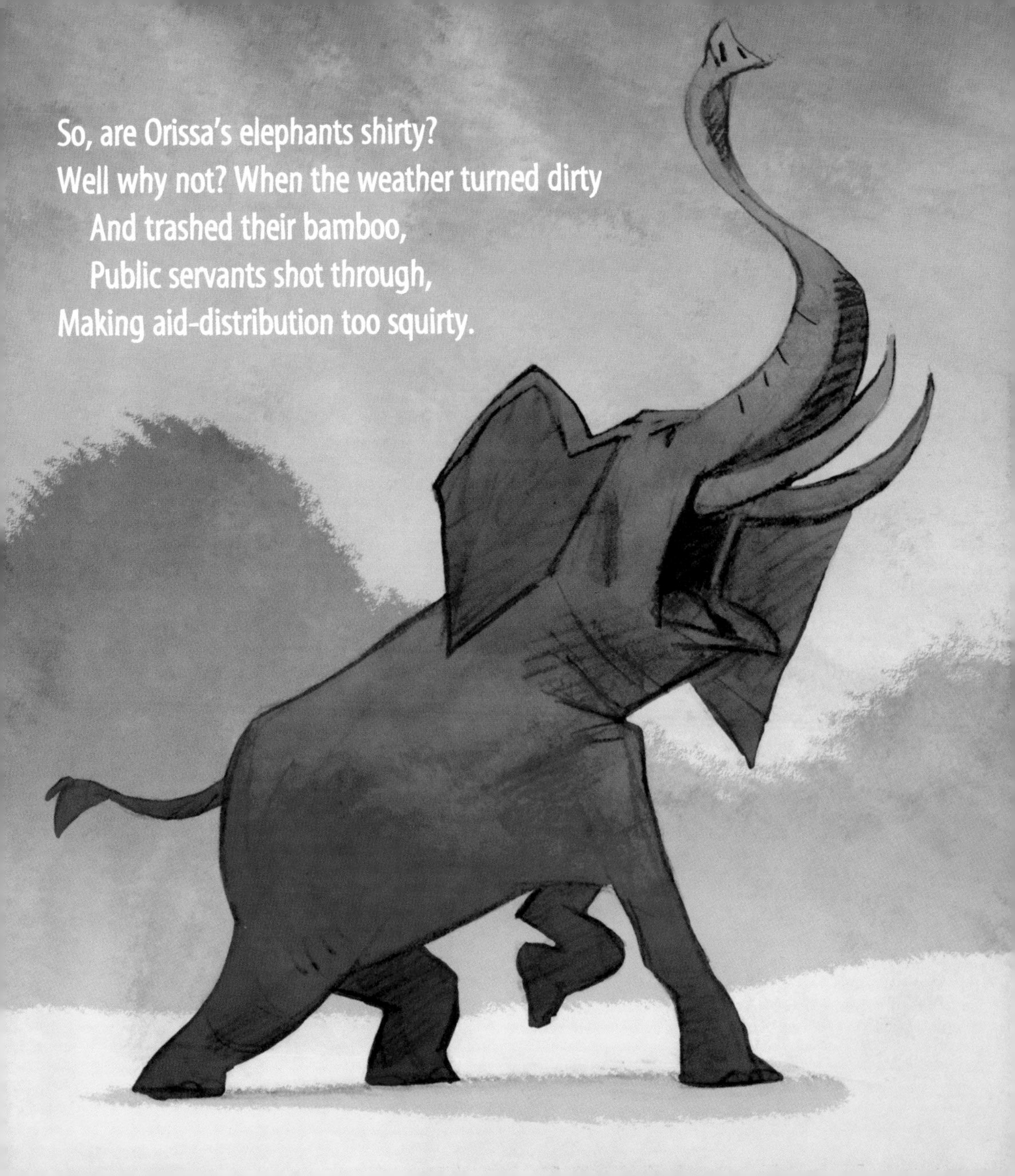

RUNAWAY ELEPHANT TAKES OVER PUBLICITY STUNT

MADRID (Reuters) — A publicity stunt by an amusement park company went awry on Wednesday when a 2-ton zoo elephant broke free from its trainer and rampaged through central Madrid during the morning rush hour.

The runaway, Clarissa, a twelve-year-old elephant, brought cars to a halt, sent pedestrians scattering in panic and knocked down two traffic signals before being felled by tranquilliser darts at the end of its 500-yard dash down a busy Madrid street.

What about what that elephant did
On a busy main street in Madrid!
Old Clarissa, in Spain,
Hit the road like a train,
But those darts stopped her dash, with a skid.

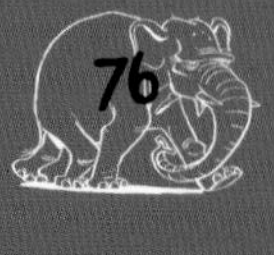

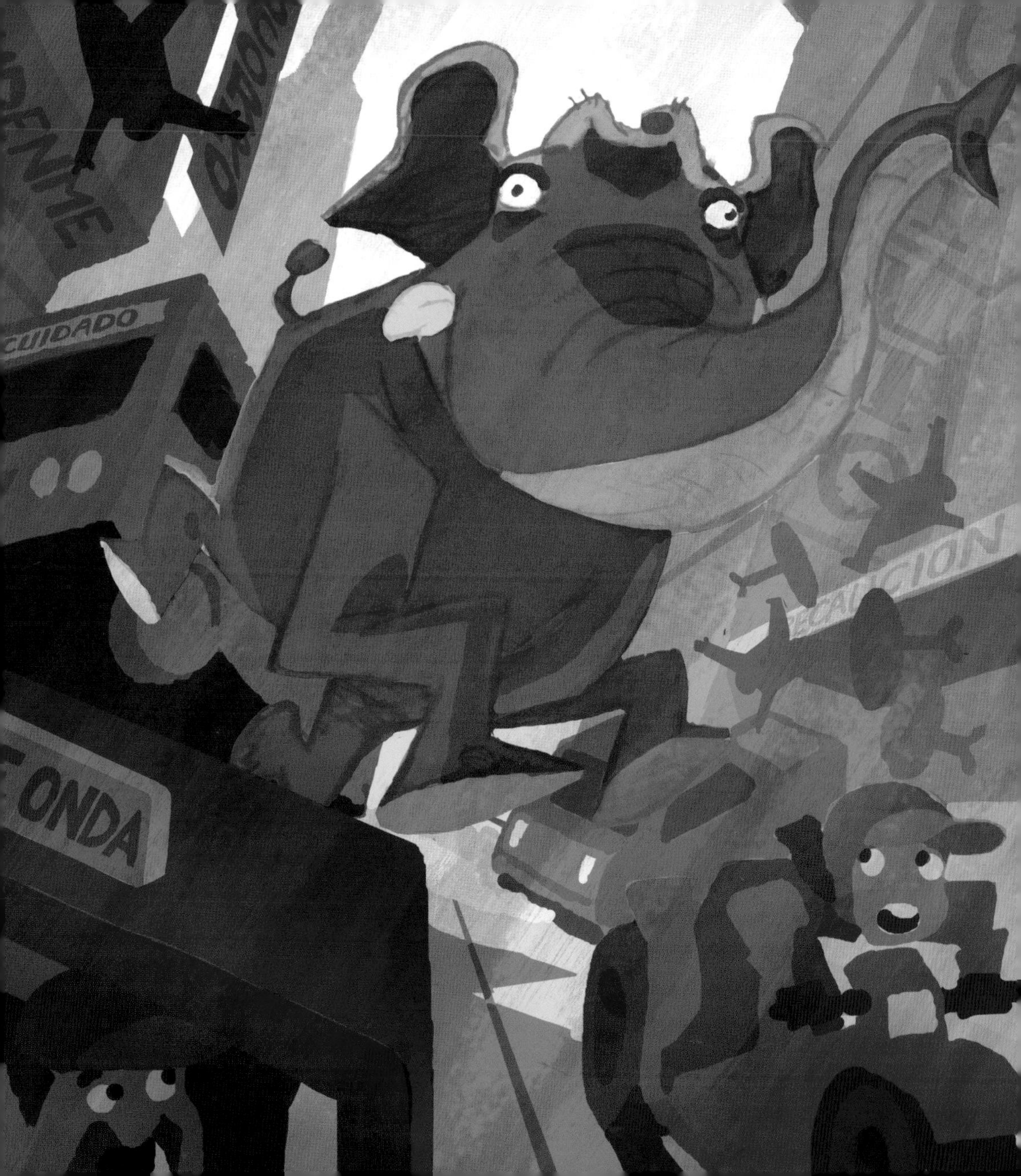
CUIDADO
ONDA

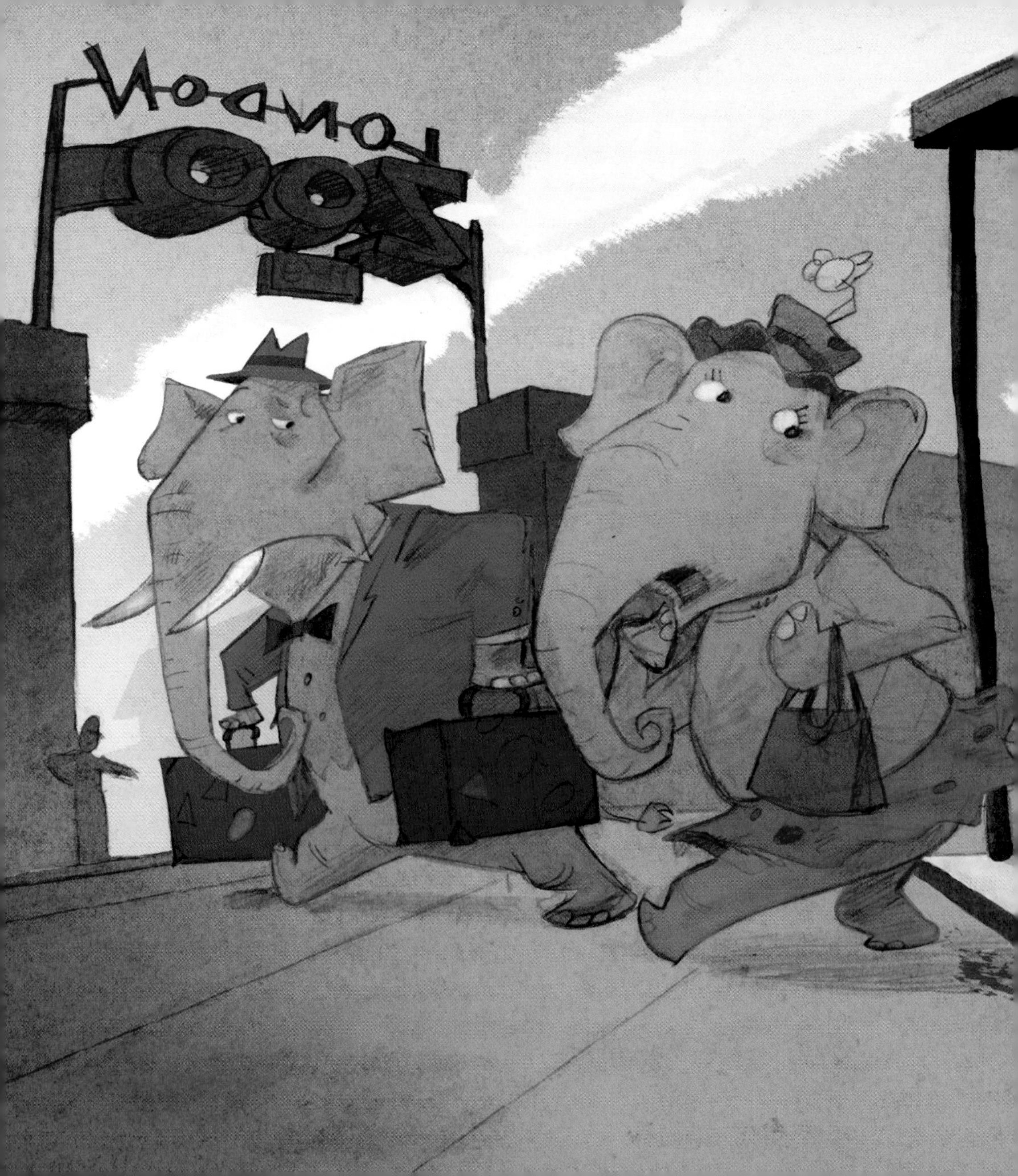
LONDON
ZOO

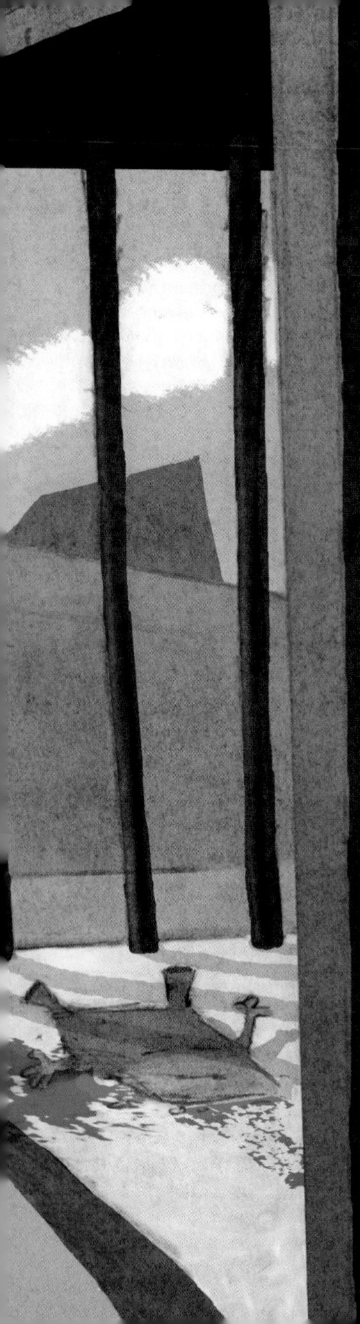

ELEPHANTS PACK THEIR TRUNKS AND SAY GOODBYE TO LONDON ZOO

Abandoning its 170-year tradition of keeping elephants has clearly been a difficult decision for London Zoo authorities, but it accords with a change in thinking about how wild animals should be kept in captivity.

The announcement was made yesterday, ten days after the death of Jim Robson, a keeper who was trampled and crushed by Dilberta, one of the three Asian elephants currently kept at the site in Regent's Park. Mr Robson had slipped and fallen inside the elephant enclosure before he was trampled to death.

Dilberta sighed, 'Yes, it sounds grim.
But I didn't know him as Jim.
I thought he was Matt;
So, when he fell flat,
I was wiping my feet clean on him.'

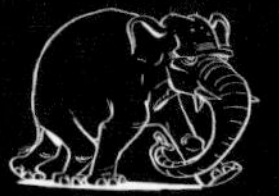

VIETNAMESE ELEPHANTS TRAMPLE SIX PEOPLE TO DEATH

A farmer has been trampled to death by wild elephants in central Vietnam. A local official in Binh Thuan province says a herd of about eight elephants pulled down a farm lookout, a 3-metre-high stilted hut, killing the 30-year-old man. In May, there was a similar incident in Binh Thuan in which two young men at a farm lookout died. A couple of weeks earlier, an elderly couple and a poacher were also killed by elephants in the same province.

Those Binh Thuan tuskers are wild;
Encroachment has got them quite riled.
    They mean to do harm,
    When the villagers farm
The forests where fodder is piled.

CRUSH ELEPHANT HAD
VIOLENT PAST

An elephant that killed a keeper at Chester Zoo was involved in other violent attacks within the past year, it has been revealed. Kumara, a 34-year-old female Asian elephant, killed senior keeper Richard Hughes.

Mr Hughes, from Stoke-on-Trent, Staffordshire, was moving the elephant from the indoor enclosure at the zoo when he was pinned to the wall by her trunk. He was due to deliver a presentation at the International Elephant and Rhinoceros Research meeting in Vienna this year.

Kumara's mind started to fester
With wrath towards her keeper in Chester,
    When report on his studies
    Would've wrecked his dear buddy's
Privacy. That so depressed her!

BRITISH TOURIST CRUSHED
IN ELEPHANT ATTACK

A British tourist was seriously ill in hospital last night after being crushed by an elephant which he had distracted from attacking his wife and friends while on safari in Botswana. Steven Street, a 32-year-old oil rig worker and lay preacher, was described as a hero for saving others in the party.

The bull elephant had rushed at the party of visitors without warning during a visit to a safari park on 25 September. Mr Street, of Nunthorpe, Middlesbrough, is reported to have waved and shouted at the animal to entice it away from the others.

A close family friend, the Rev. Alan Leighton, of St George's Church, Normanby, Middlesbrough, praised Mr Street's bravery. 'He is still fighting for his life, although we are now hopeful that he will pull through. Steven is a lovely man, a real church leader. This is a terrible thing to have happened.'

A good Christian hero named Steve
Saved people from elephant's peeve.
The mystery was why
It charged such a nice guy.
Perhaps it just doesn't believe.

82

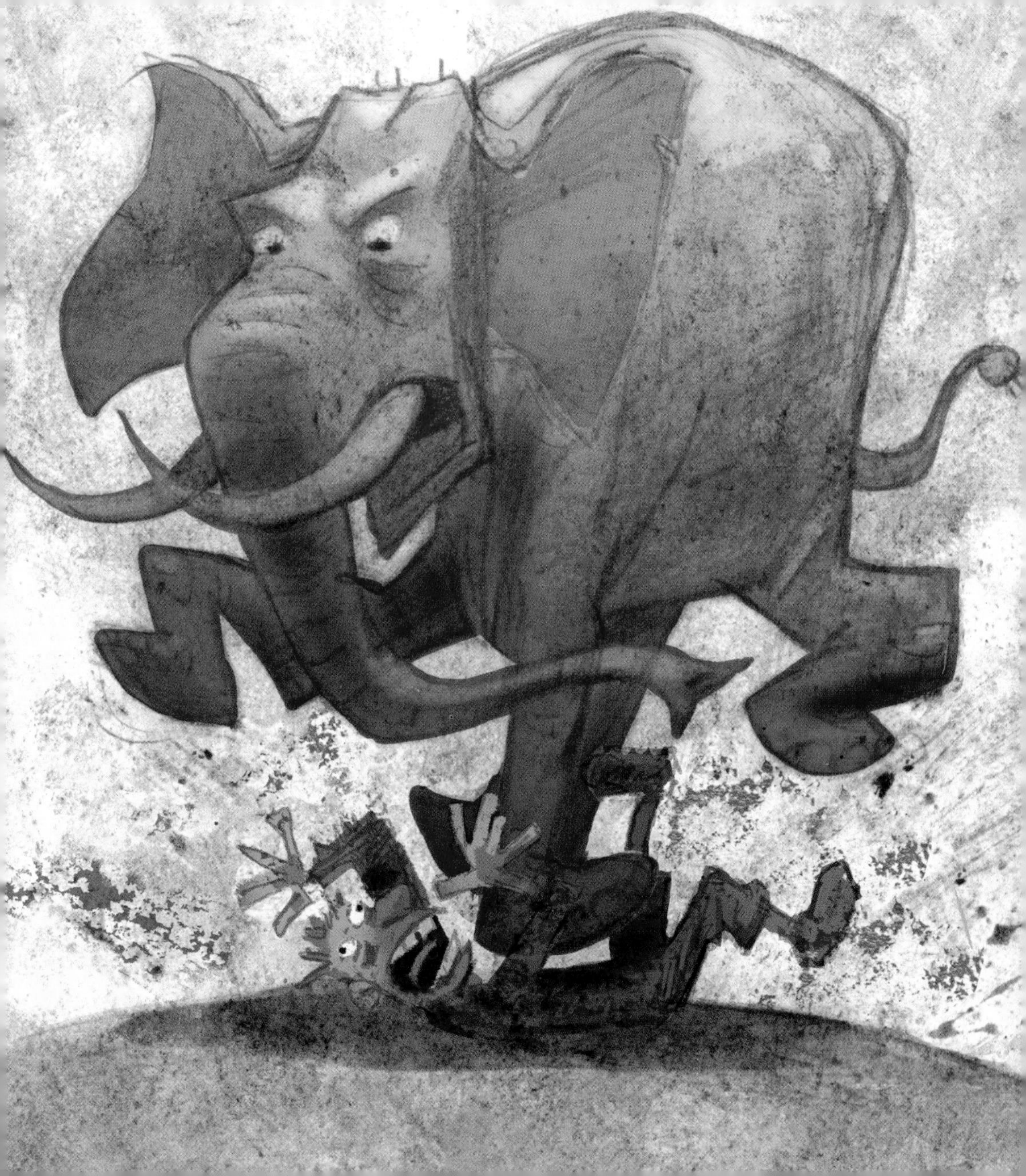

JOURNALIST
TRAMPLED TO DEATH
BY ELEPHANT IN CHINA

A journalist in China has been attacked and trampled to death by a
wild elephant while on an assignment in southwestern Yunnan
province. The journalist was shooting footage of crop damage caused
by elephants when the elephant managed to cross a ditch dug to
protect people and crushed the man to death.

One more of wild elephants' crimes
That with 'Man Bites Dog' news item chimes:
   We read, with our feet up,
   That a scribe copped a beat-up.
(Would he have, if he'd worked for *The Times*?)

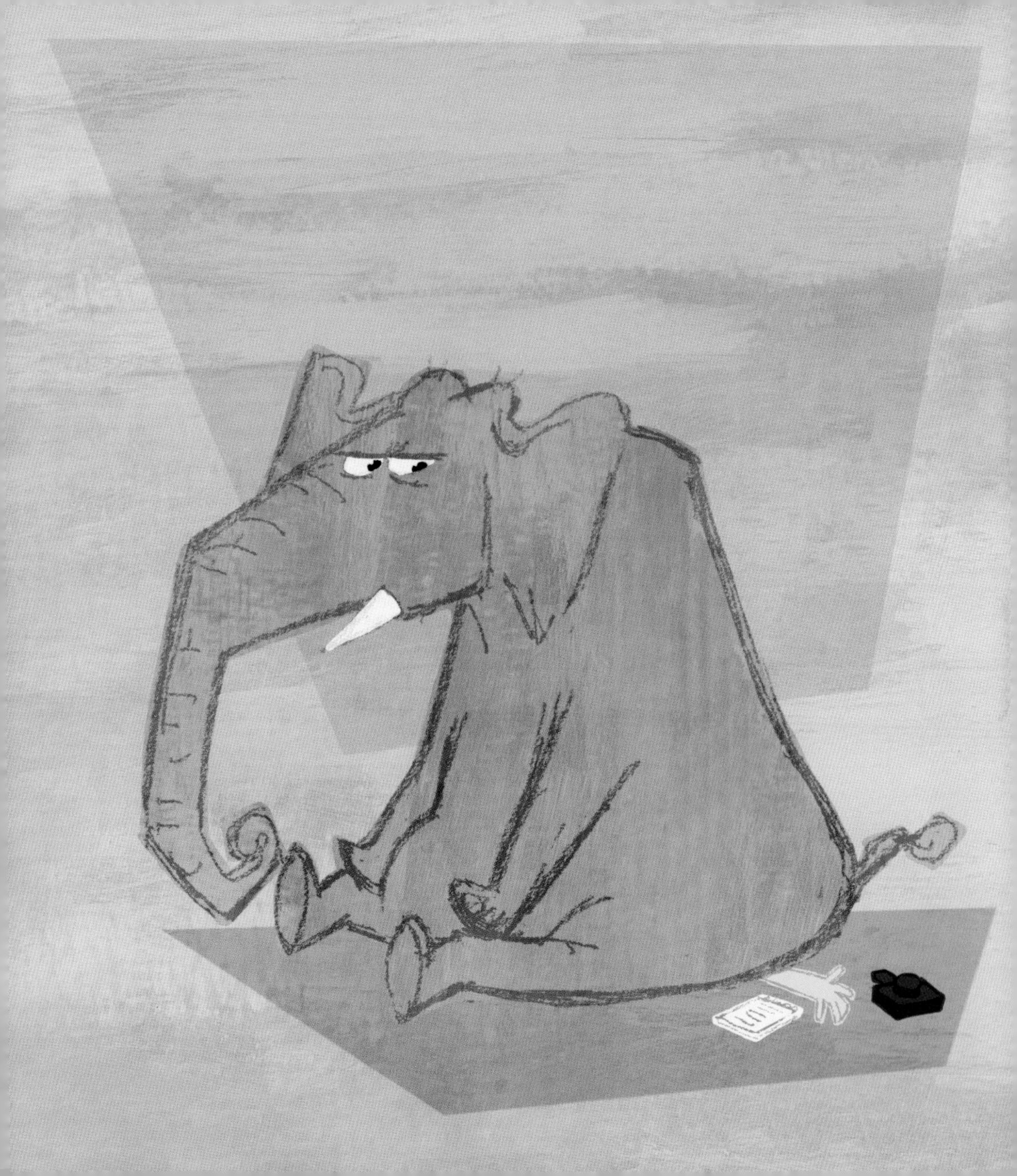

ELEPHANT TRAMPLES MAN AND KEEPS THE CORPSE

GUWAHATI, India (Reuters) — A wild elephant pulled a man down from a tree, trampled him to death and for two weeks has refused to part with the corpse, police in northeast India say.

The man climbed the tree to escape a herd of wild elephants rampaging through his village about 80 miles from Guwahati, the largest city in Assam. 'The elephant must have got even more irritated as the villagers were trying to free the man,' a forest ranger said on Sunday. 'It trampled him to death and took the body along with him.'

That was two weeks ago and it has been carrying the body around ever since, police said.

'Good Lord!' the wild elephant said;
'Why wonder I've kept him, though dead?
   There's no use at all
   In the corpse. But my wall
Will look nice when I've mounted the head!'

86

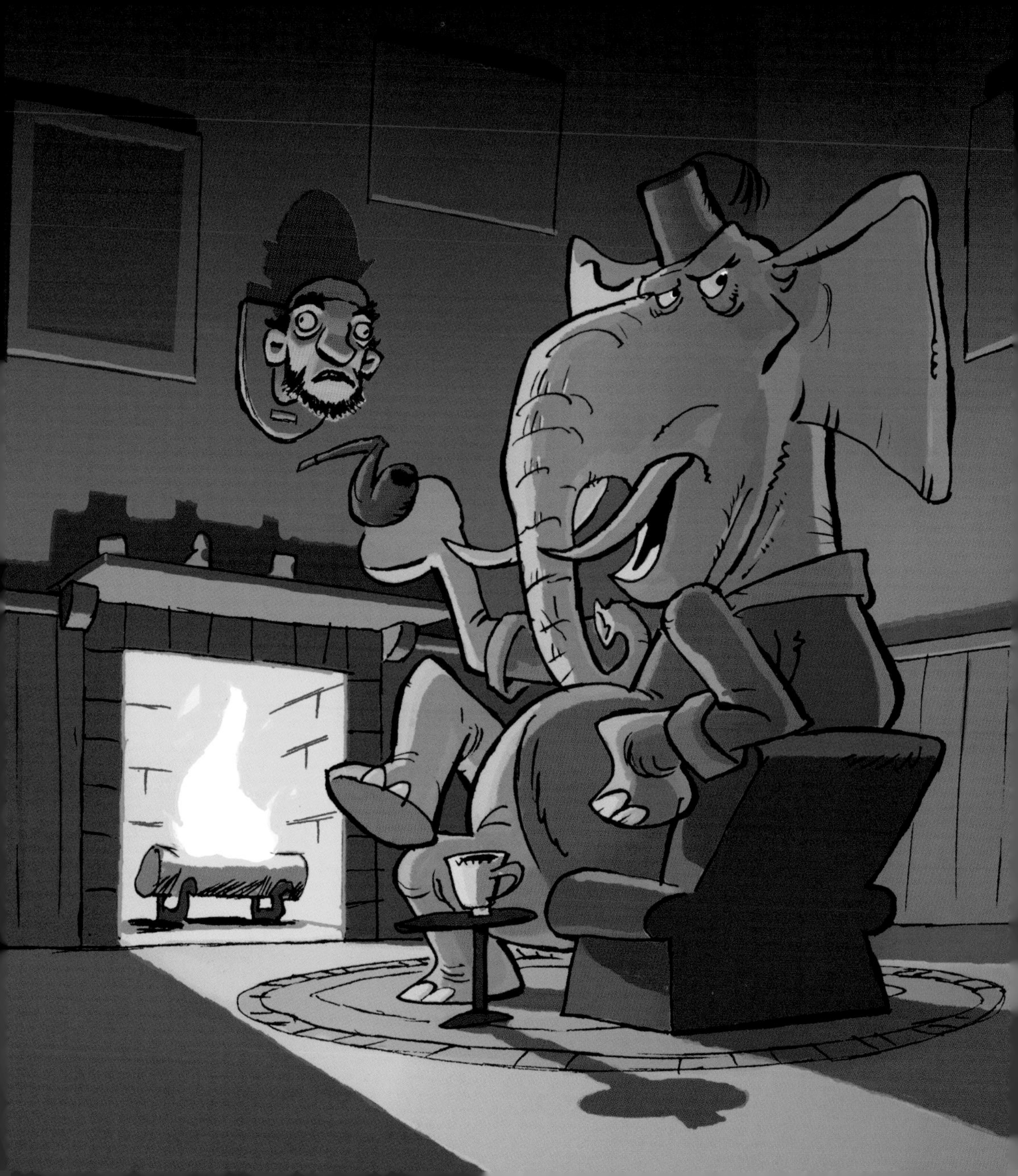

CHAPTER SIX:
ELEPHANTS UNDER THE GUN

'With poachers all drawing a bead on
    Us elephants, no time for hedonistic delay
    In our feeding and play!
We'd better be clapping more speed on.'

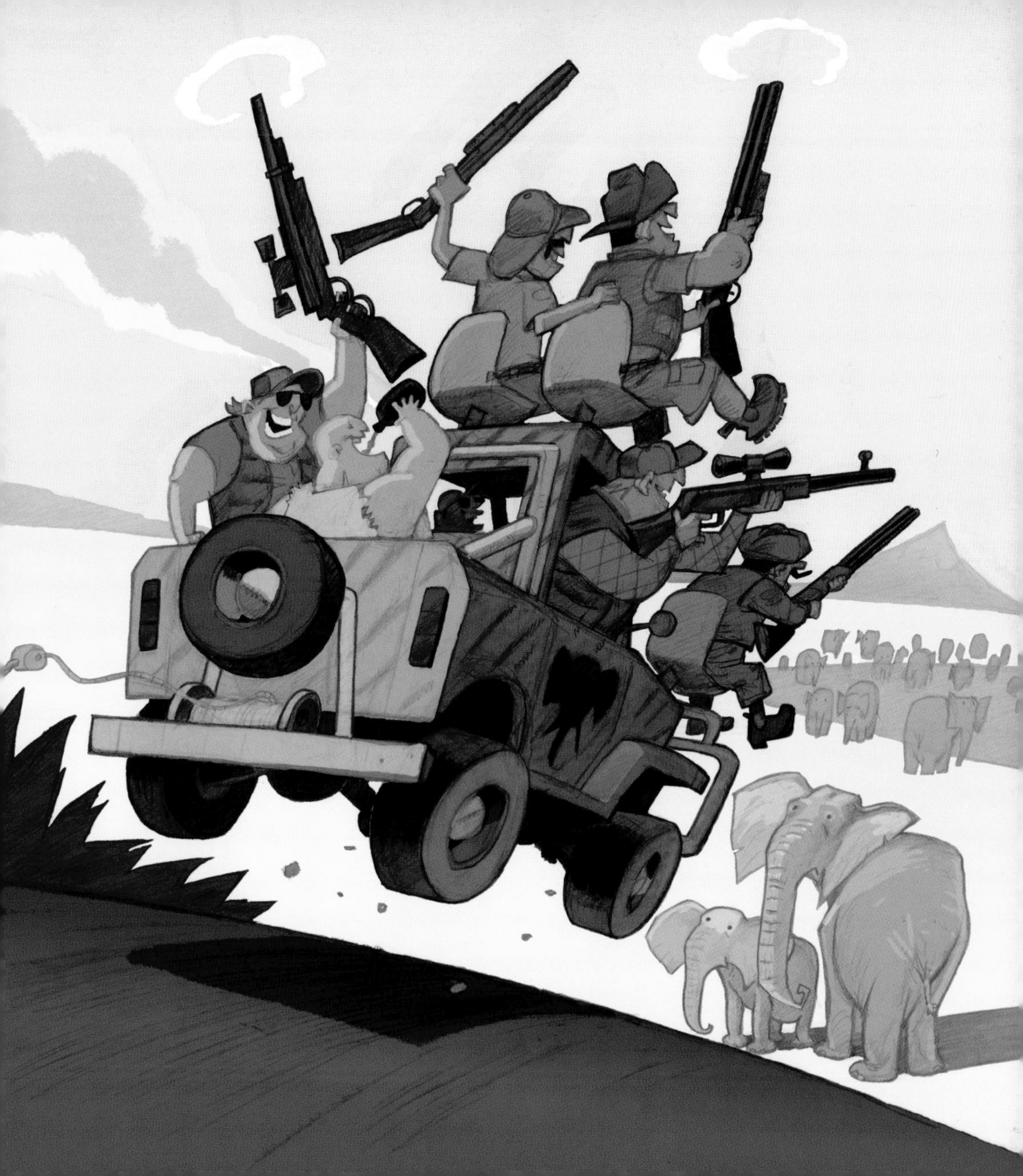

ELEPHANTS EAT THEIR WAY TO EQUILIBRIUM

Research by a UK-based scientist suggests that African elephant breeding rates are determined by their environment. Contrary to popular belief, he says, the elephants do not breed beyond the carrying capacity of their habitat. Their reproductive capacity is automatically checked. And the result is a finely balanced system which avoids any need for human adjustments.

An elephant cull? What a laugh!
Those tuskers don't do things by half.
When feed's running short,
Each cow knows she ought
To stop from producing a calf.

CONFIDENT ELEPHANTS NUDGE INTO NAIROBI

Emboldened by Kenya's success in stamping out poaching, elephants have started wandering into the suburbs of Nairobi for the first time for more than a century.

A bull thus straying was recently anaesthetised by a dart from a helicopter, winched onto a truck, and taken 240 kilometres back to Amboseli park.

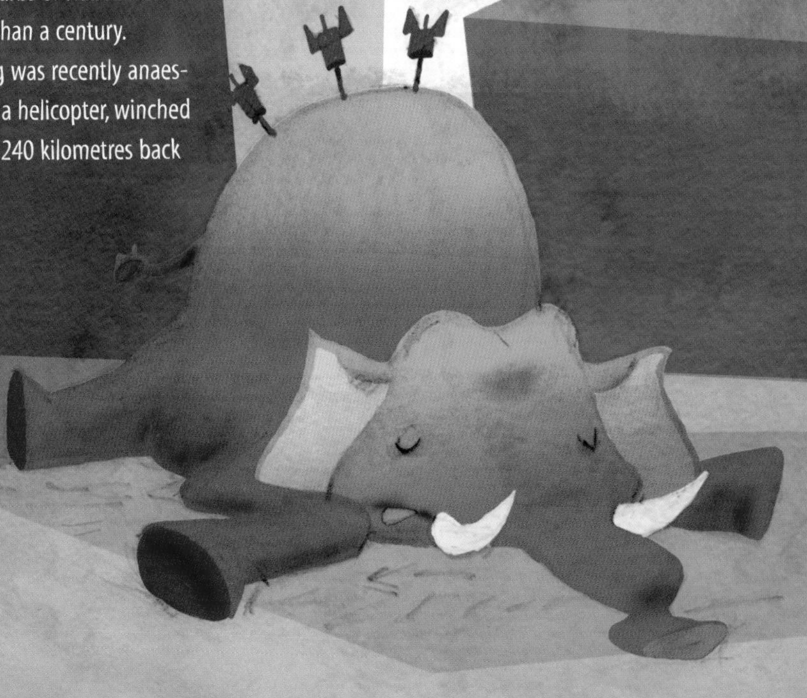

'It's safe in the city for me,'
Laughed the Nairobi tusker with glee.
Then, with dart, truck, and winch,
Comes an elephant pinch;
And he's back in his park before tea!

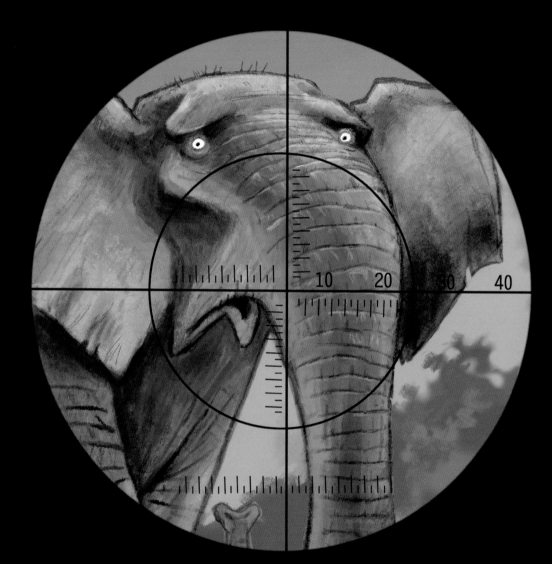

POACHERS HAVE CREATED BREED OF TUSKLESS ELEPHANT

Ivory poaching may be causing Asian elephants to lose the gene that allows them to develop tusks, conservationists claim. Not all male Asian elephants grow tusks. The ones that do are the ones being hunted by ivory poachers, so the tusk gene may well disappear from the population.

About 40 to 50 per cent of the animals are normally tuskless, but in Sri Lanka it has been found recently that more than 90 per cent of the population are not growing tusks, perhaps because of the poaching effect.

Said the World Wide Fund spokesman, 'Cor lumme!
Genetic mutations are rummy.
What with poaching (obscene!)
And recessive tusk gene,
Our elephants could end up gummy.'

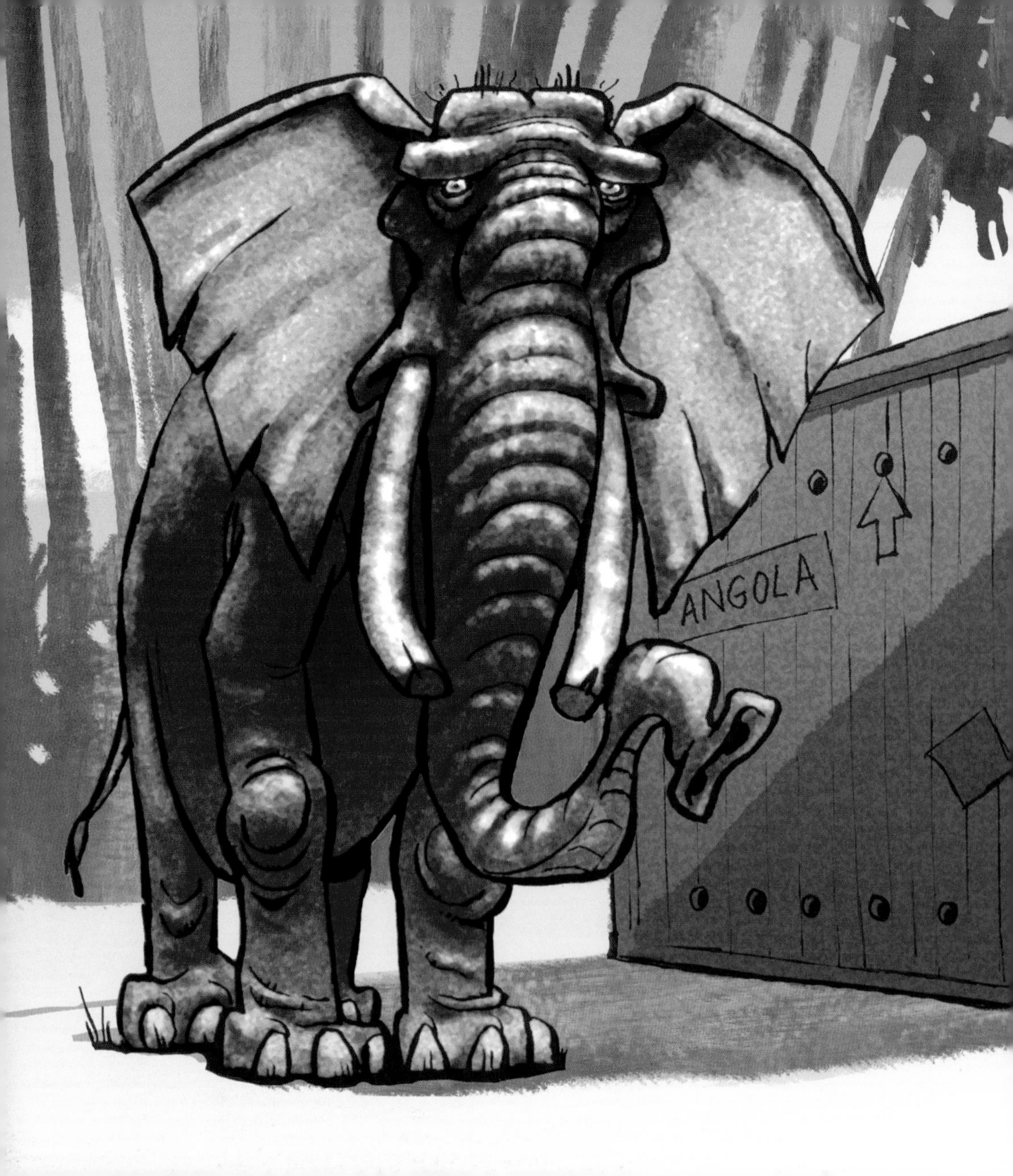
ANGOLA

JUMBOS JET IN TO ANGOLA

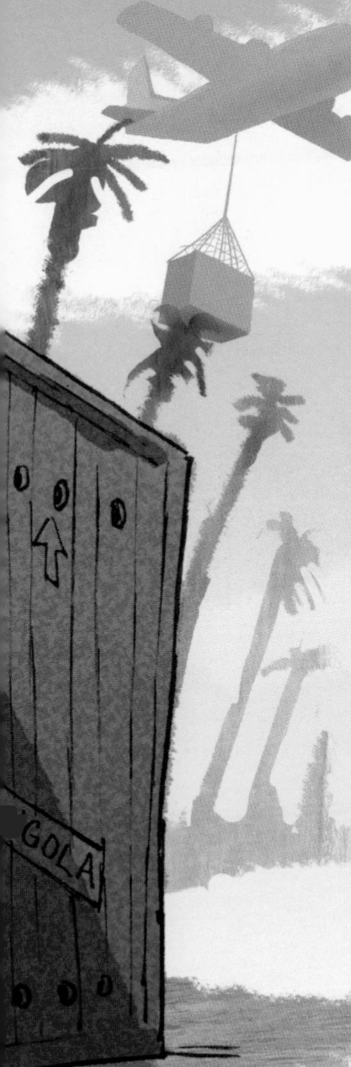
GOLA

A planeload of elephants are now getting used to their new home in one of Angola's war-ravaged game parks, after being flown in from South Africa. The eight elephants, part of 300 donated by Botswana, arrived in specially adapted shipping containers and have been released into Quicama National Park on the Angola coast.

In addition to the immense human cost of 25 years of civil war, the Angolan conflict has also taken its toll on the country's wildlife stocks. Animals were driven away by fighting or killed for food by rival armies.

The first airlift of animals to replenish the game stock in Angola took place a year ago when 30 elephants were flown in.

Mused an Angola tusker to me,
'Time's whirlygig's something to see!
One day, come the crunch,
You're a guerrilla's lunch;
The next, a flown-in VIP.'

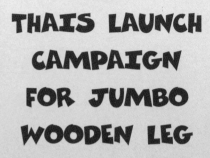

THAIS LAUNCH CAMPAIGN FOR JUMBO WOODEN LEG

A public appeal has been launched to buy a wooden leg for an elephant which stepped on a landmine near the Thai border with Burma earlier this month. Vets say Motala, a 38-year-old jumbo, is in a stable condition but is likely to need her leg amputated.

The Friends of the Asian Elephant Foundation says it has asked people to dip into their pockets to find the $27,000 needed to treat Motala and buy her a massive prosthesis.

To those Thai vets I'd simply say, 'Fellas!
For mending Motala as well as
She was pre the bang,
Just teach her the hang
Of a grafted-on stand for umbrellas.'

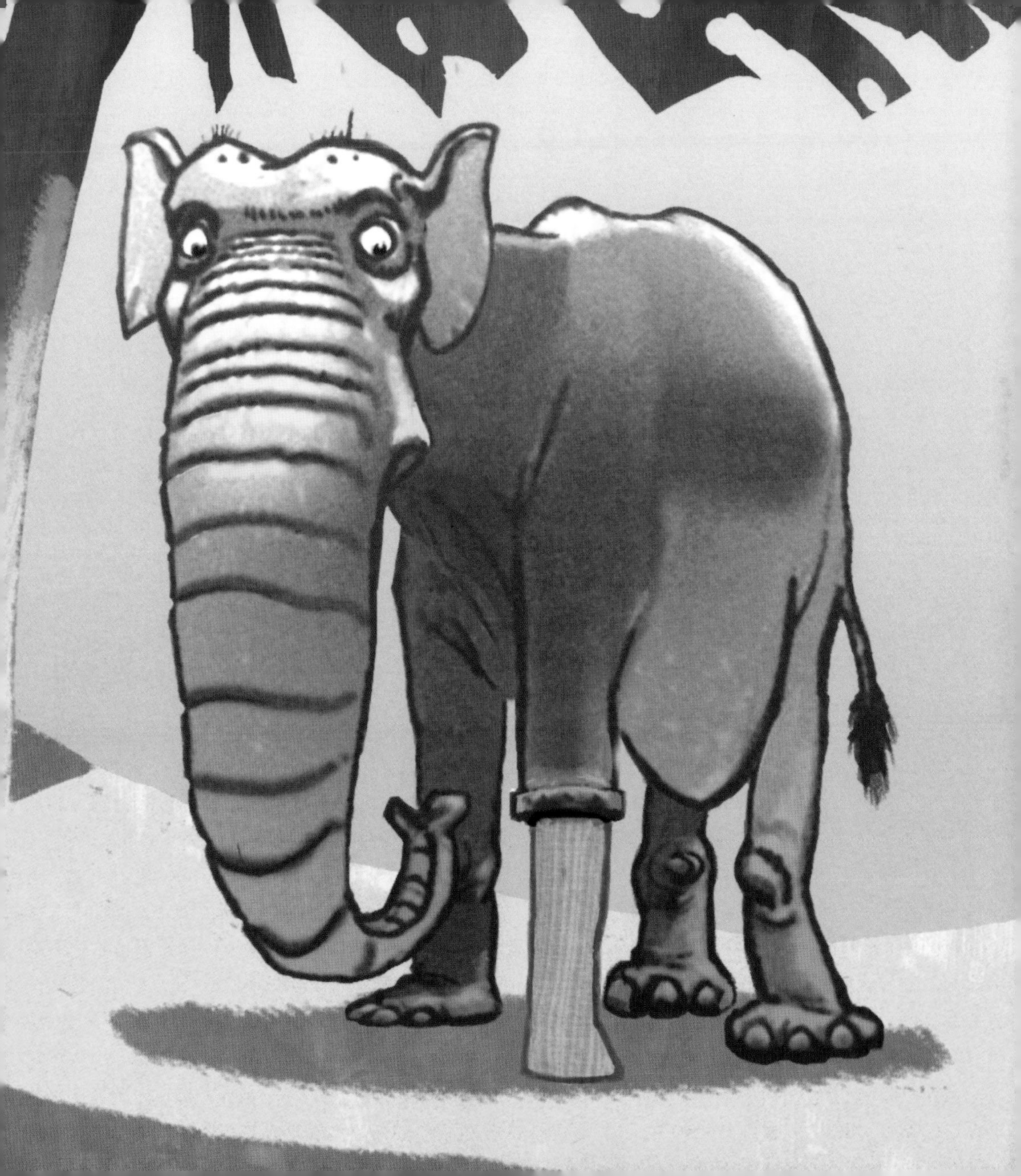

A JUMBO-SIZED DILEMMA IN ZAMBIA

Village headman Redson Zimba walks through what used to be a banana plantation. A few nights ago, a herd of elephants paid a visit to his settlement. They snapped the banana trees, ate the maize crops, and trampled through the village looking for mangoes. In his view, elephants are nothing but giant vermin.

Marianthe Noble, the country representative of the British conservation charity, the David Shepherd Foundation, believes that the growing human population should be shifted out of the Luangwa Valley.

'They were never there in the first place,' says Mrs Noble. 'They should move them back to where they belong. Why should everyone live in a game park?'

98

Marianthe states, 'Come to the crunch,
I'd sooner the Zambians lacked lunch.
  Life on tusker reserve
  Mankind just don't deserve;
They're such an expendable bunch!'

SURGE IN ZIMBABWE ELEPHANT POACHING

There has been a dramatic upsurge in elephant poaching in Zimbabwe, one of the countries allowed to sell ivory stocks earlier this year.

The new figures come from the country's state-owned newspaper, the *Herald*, and so can be treated as semi-official. The paper says that in Chewore National Park, 84 elephants have been killed this year — 31 of them in the past fortnight.

Trade in ivory was banned ten years ago after poaching decimated elephant populations in much of Africa. But in April this year, three countries which had managed to preserve their elephant herds, sold their ivory stocks to Japan on an experimental basis.

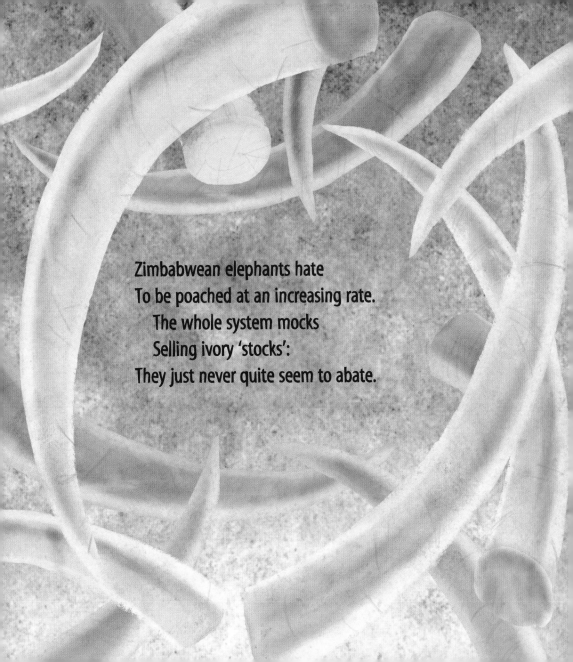

Zimbabwean elephants hate
To be poached at an increasing rate.
The whole system mocks
Selling ivory 'stocks':
They just never quite seem to abate.

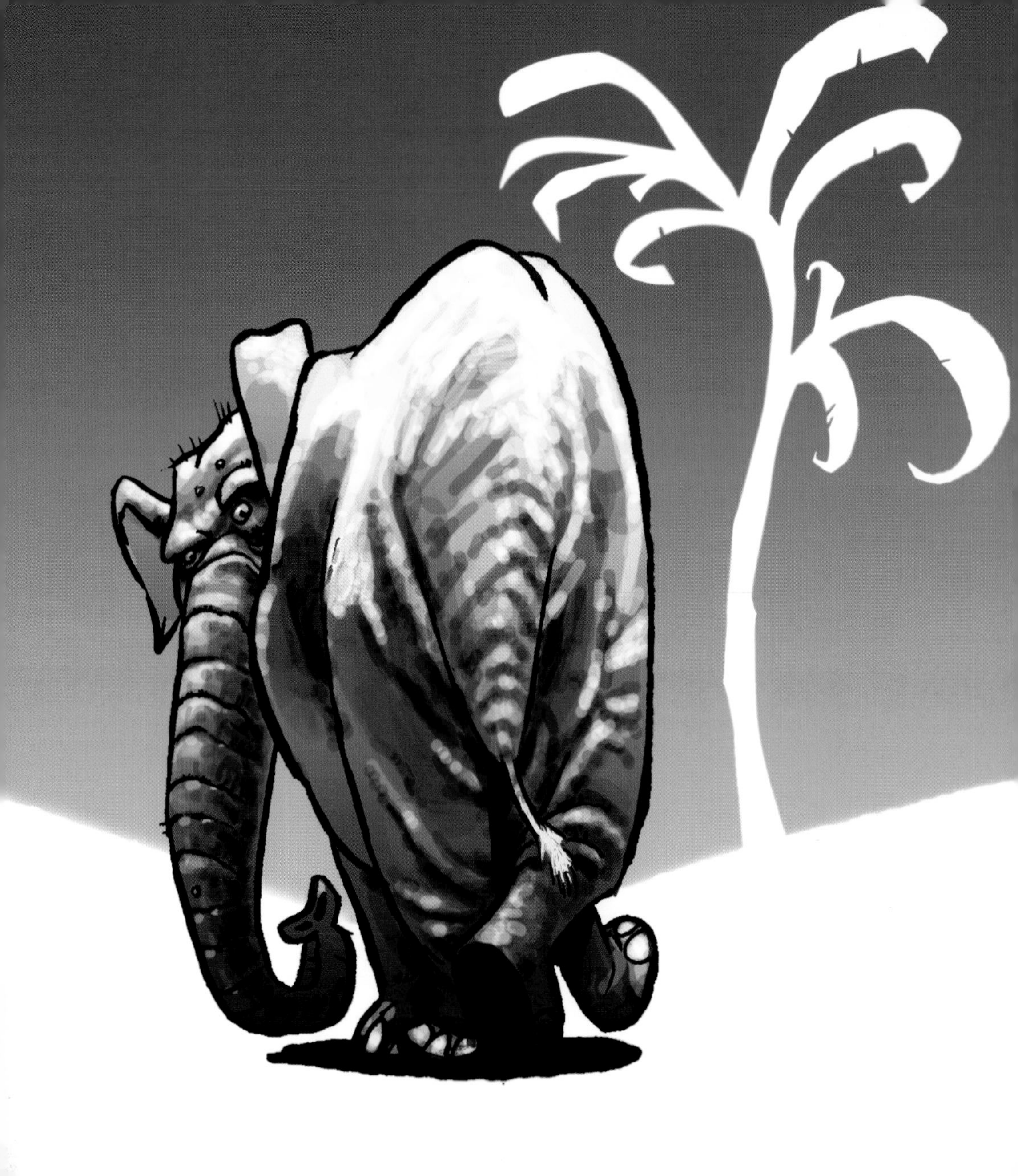

ELEPHANTS HUNTED FOR HAIR ON THEIR TAILS

COLOMBO (Reuters) — Elephants are killed in Sri Lanka for the hair on their tails due to an ancient legend that it gives man the power of the animal. A single strand of elephant hair could fetch up to 2000 rupees ($29) if sold to foreigners.

Old elephants do become frail,
Scarce worthy of 'Dogmeat for sale!'
But still it's the truth
That we're hunted. Forsooth,
On the strength of the hair on our tail.

ELEPHANT FORESTS WILL BE BUGGED

Microphones are to be deployed in African forests to eavesdrop on elephants. Researchers hope that the system, which will link an array of microphones to satellites, will act as an early warning network to protect the animals from farmers and poachers.

An array of four or more microphones will allow scientists to work out the position of animals in a forest and the direction in which they are travelling.

Steve Guilick, a recording engineer in the Cornell team, said: 'At the moment, we can find out about poaching activity only after the carnage, when we're walking through the carcasses.'

The monitoring scheme is partly funded by the World Wildlife Fund. A spokesman for the university said that, if the work proves successful, the researchers envisage deploying hundreds in forests across Africa to protect more herds from poachers.

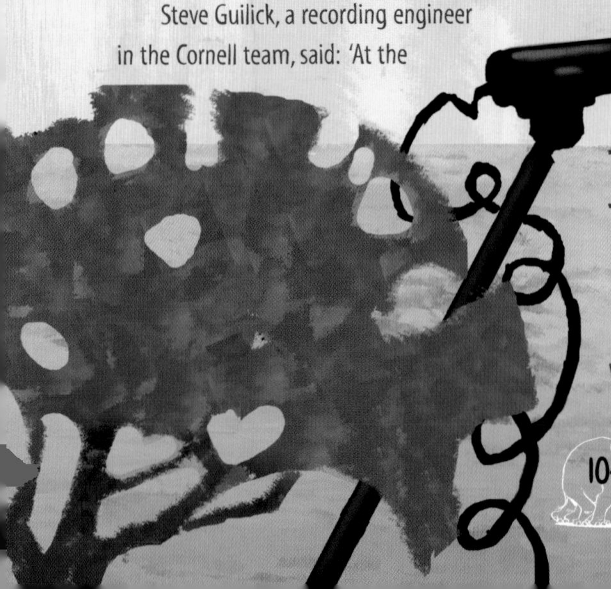

The elephants cry, 'Is it fair
That we can't be safe in our lair?
It's really too much!
All these warnings and such
Will work only while we're on air.'

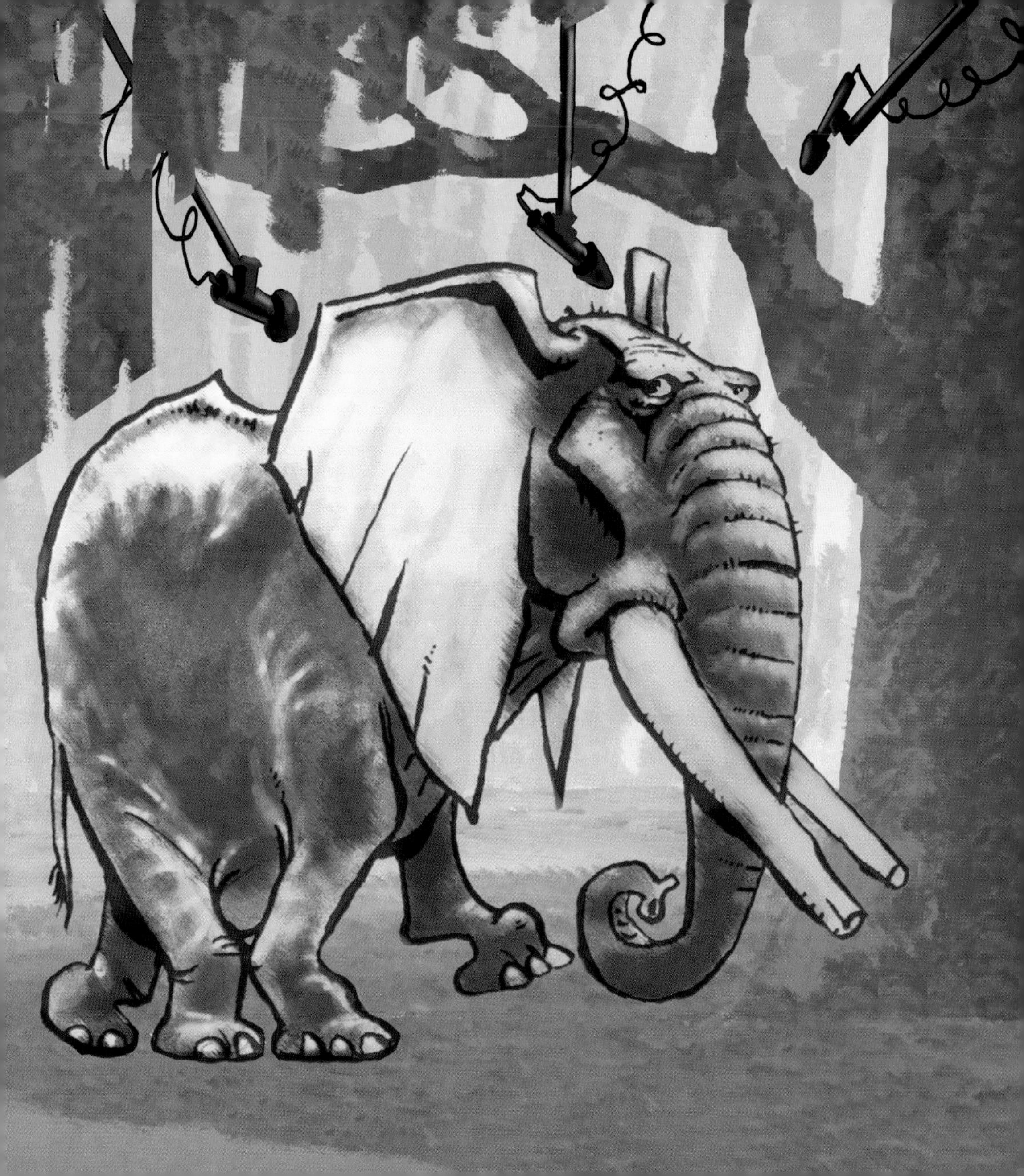

CHAPTER SEVEN:
ELEPHANTS IN THE ARTS

Sighed a tusker, 'I'm rank amateur
About culture. This may cause a stir:
Don't know much about art;
But, deep down in my heart,
I do know which kinds I prefer.'

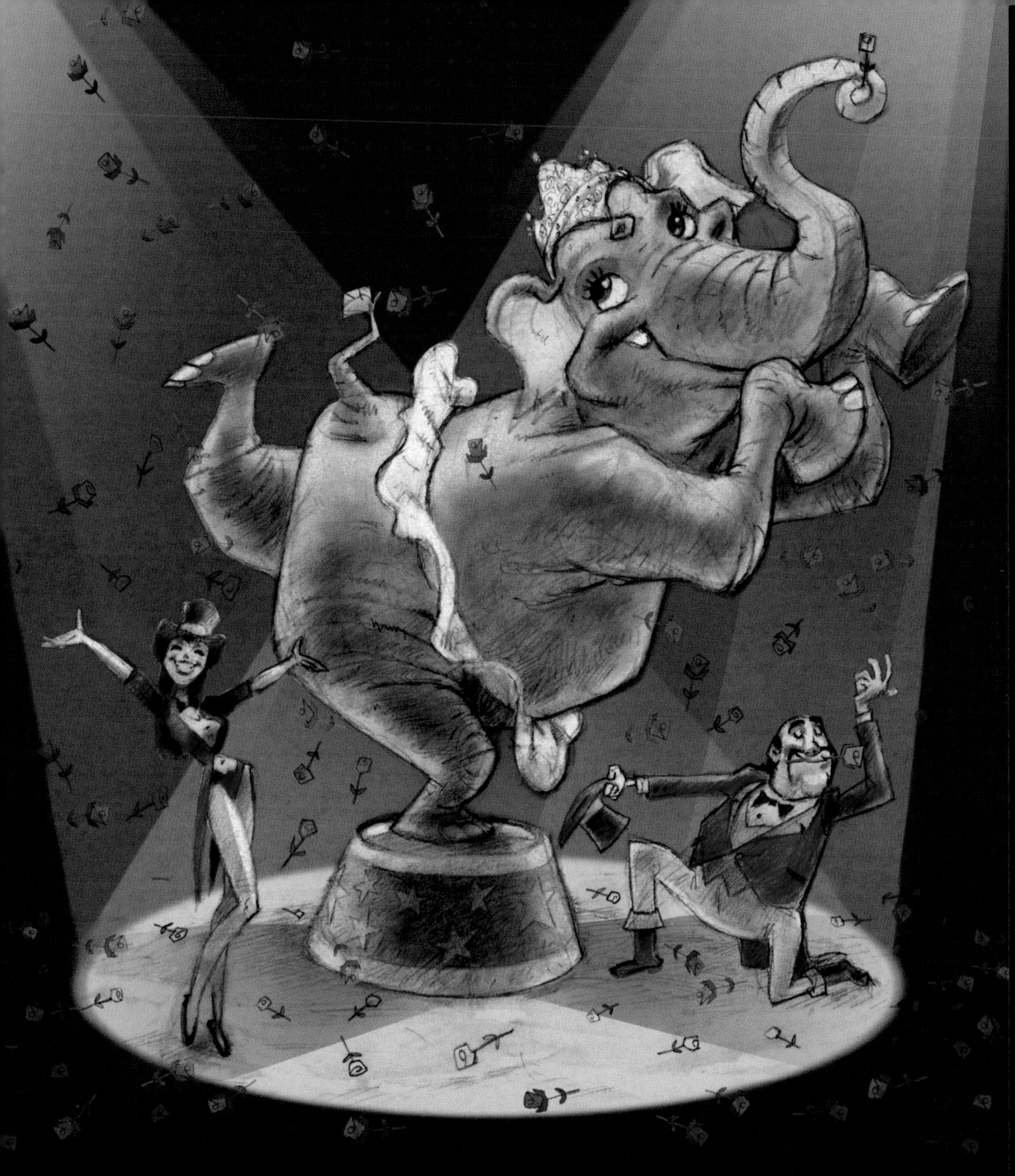

GIULIANI MAY COUNTER-SUE OVER NEW YORK ART SHOW

WASHINGTON (Reuters) — New York Mayor Rudolph Giuliani threatened on Sunday to sue personally the Brooklyn Museum of Art over a controversial art show that includes a portrait of the Virgin Mary with a clump of elephant dung stuck to it.

The city filed a lawsuit on Thursday seeking to revoke the museum's lease for the city-owned building and evict it from the site. Then on Friday, it withheld a $500,000 funding payment for the museum, which gets $7 million a year from the city. Earlier in the week, the museum sued Giuliani personally in Brooklyn federal court, asking that he be barred from withholding funds from the museum over the exhibit.

108

They're saying, 'Oh man, this is scary.
What His Honour has done is unfair! He
   Has turned off the tap,
   Because elephant crap
And some porn cutouts say "Virgin Mary".'

ELEPHANT PAINTERS

Prominent New York City artists Vitaly Komar and Alex Melamid went to Thailand to teach elephants to paint so their works could be sold to support the elephants and their masters, out of work since the forest logging industry that employed them was outlawed. Placing a print of a work by renowned abstract expressionist Willem de Kooning alongside a similar-looking painting from the trunk of an elephant named Lukop, Melamid says the two examples are 'absolutely' in the same genre.

The Art lecturer moaned to his class,
'Tuskers painting? Oh hell, what a farce!
Holding brush in their trunk,
They daub nothing but junk.
Might as well shove the brush up their arse!'

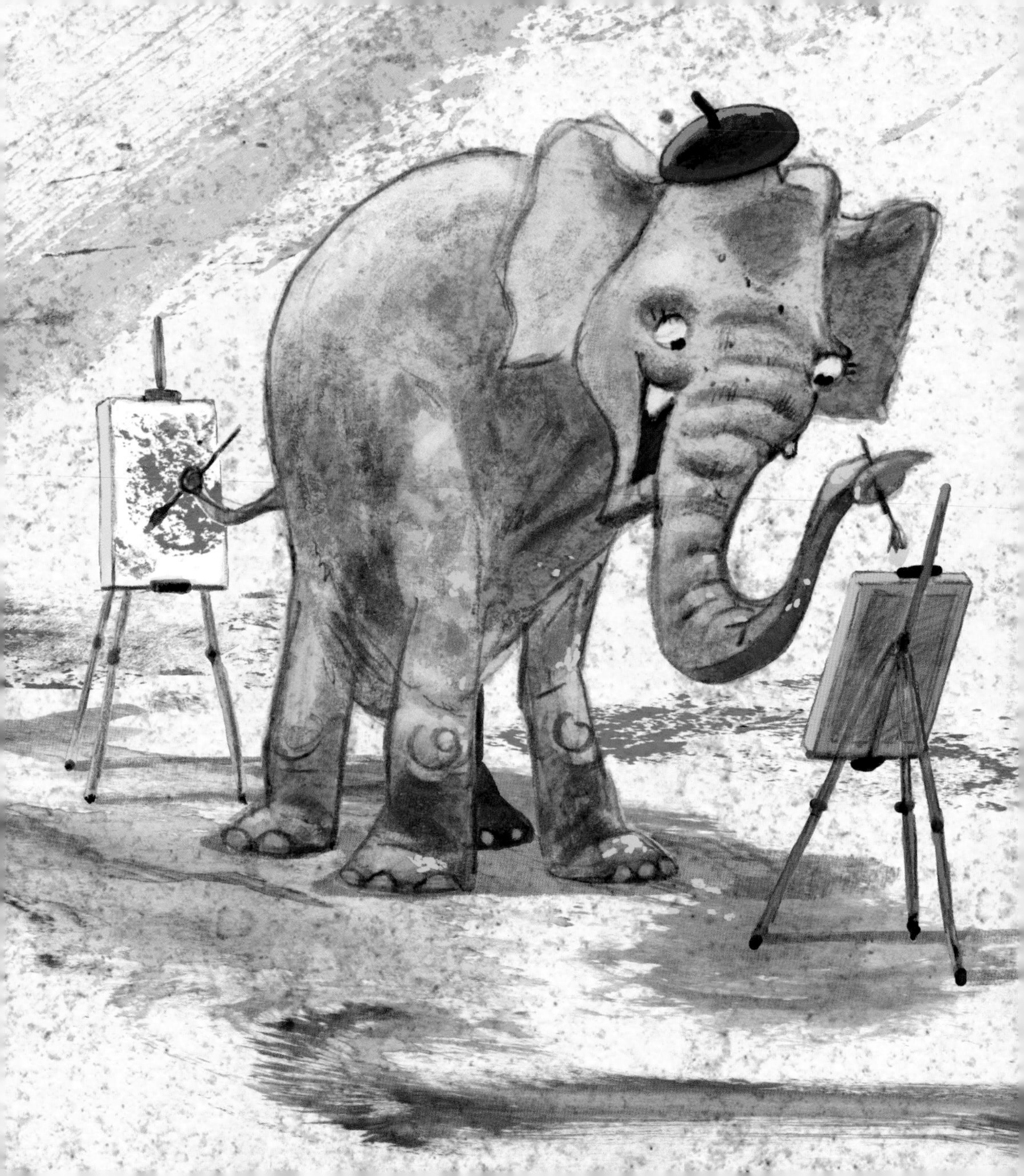

ARTFUL ELEPHANTS REWARDED

Turner Prize-winning artist Chris Ofili, whose works have often employed dung contributed by elephants from London Zoo, is returning the compliment.

The artist is donating a painting to the Zoological Society of London (ZSL). The painting 'Triple Couple' will be auctioned this week at New York's contemporary art fair The Armory, and is expected to fetch some £40,000.

The proceeds will go to the elephants at Whipsnade Wild Animal Park — where the last remaining elephants from London Zoo were transferred last year.

Those tuskers at Whipsnade Zoo, Beds.,
Are helplessly shaking their heads:
 'Dear Chris, call it quits;
 Your daubs in our shits
Are what an art-lover most dreads.'

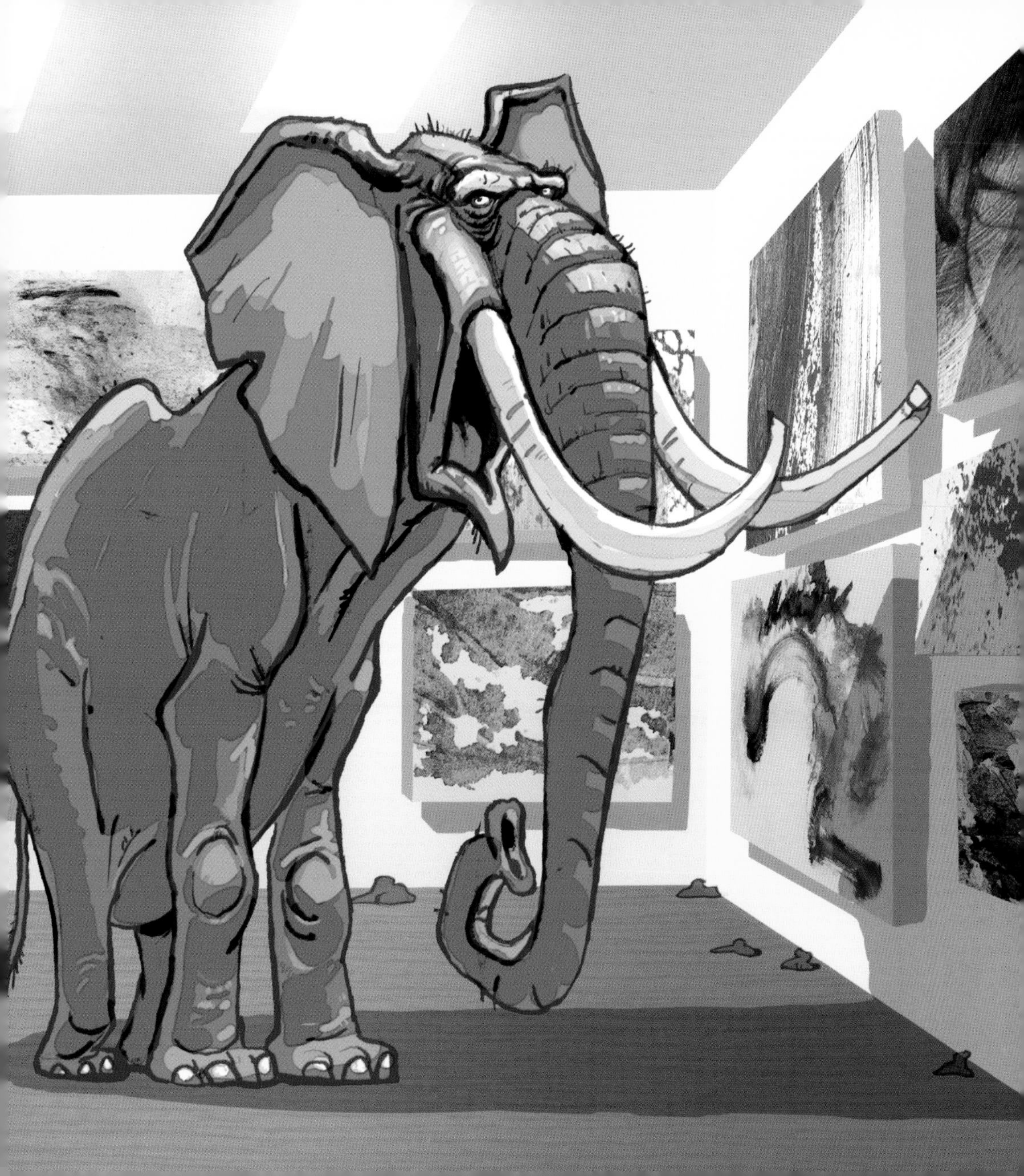

SOUTH AFRICAN GAME PARK OFFERS NOVEL MEMENTO

KNYSNA, South Africa (Reuters) — Visitors to Knysna Elephant Park about 300 miles east of Cape Town can take home a unique memento of their visit.

Park owners Ian and Lisette Withers are offering dried, vacuum-packed elephant dung — priced at $2.40 for a clear, plastic container the size of a small coffee cup. 'It sells. I don't know what people do with it. But it sells,' Ian Withers told Reuters.

114

Does life make you age — all gone bung,
When you'd like to stay vital and young?
All is right in a jiff
If you just take a whiff
Of a pack of dried elephant dung.

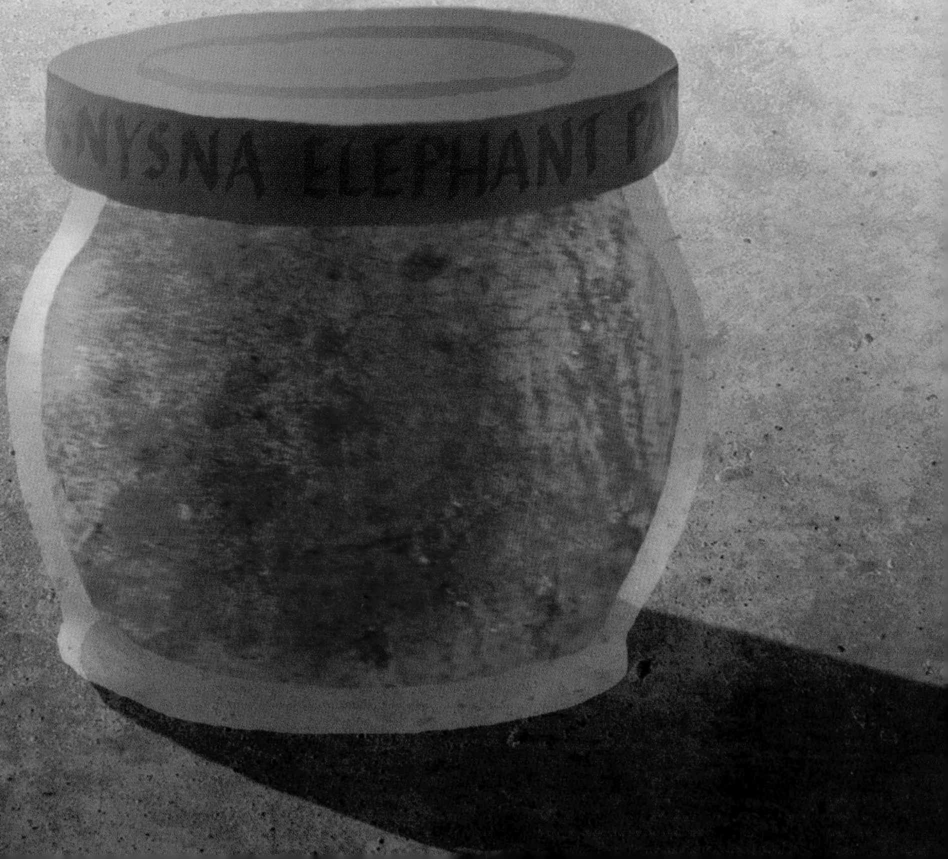
NYSNA ELEPHANT

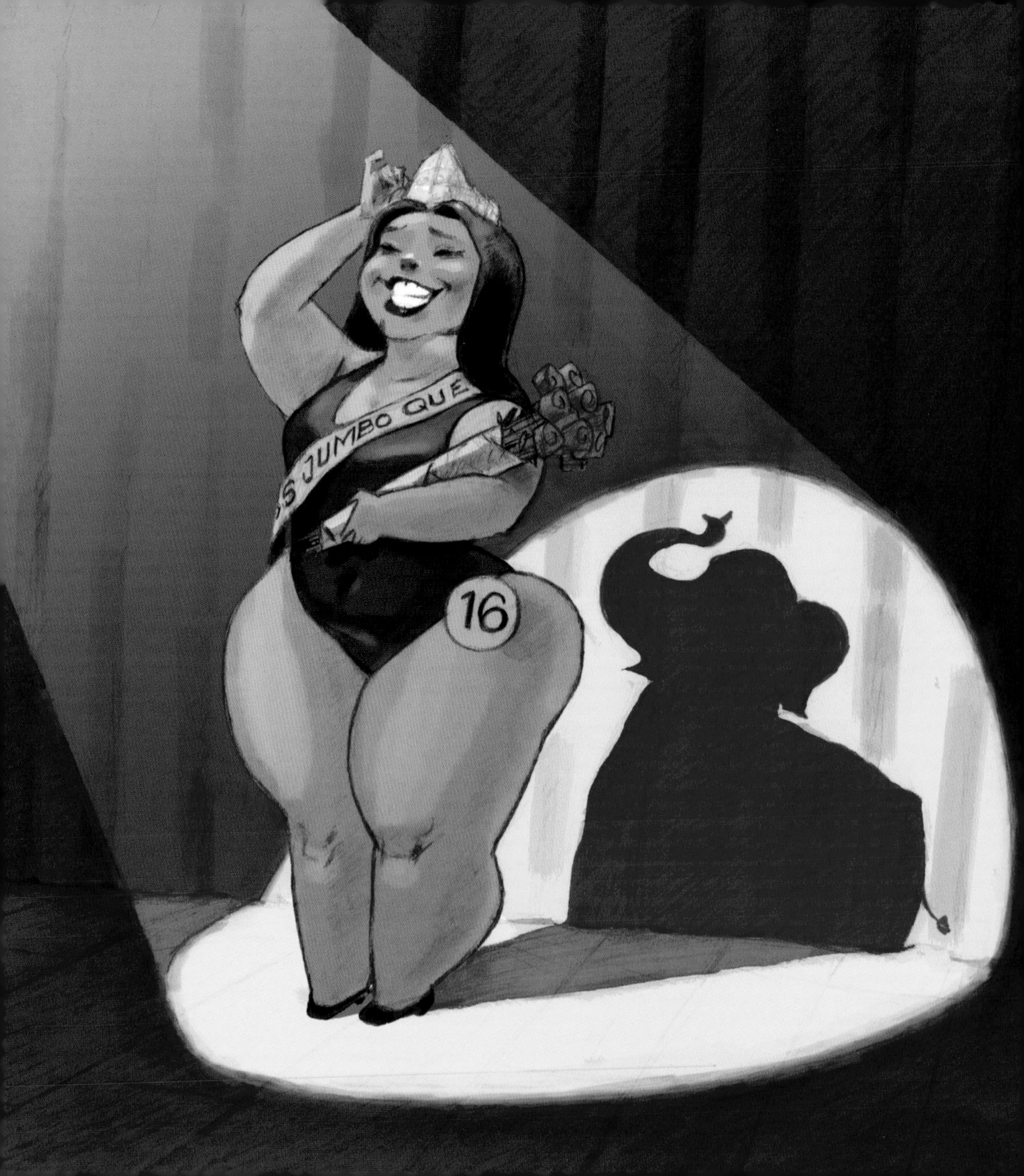
S JUMBO QUE
16

THAILAND CROWNS 'MISS JUMBO QUEEN'

One month before Bangkok hosts the Miss Universe competition, Thailand has crowned a 110-kilogram business student winner of a light-hearted, heavyweight pageant staged to promote elephant conservation. The annual event is an unlikely precursor to the international pageant on 30 May in Bangkok, but the Jumbo Queen has become a strangely popular event.

In a nod to the upcoming Miss Universe pageant, a special Miss Jumbo Universe prize was awarded to the heaviest contestant — Thanchanok Mekkeaw, a 25-year-old political science student who was weighed on-stage at 182 kilograms. Women aged 18–35 are eligible to enter, as long as they weigh at least 80 kilos. Judges score the women not only on their performances and an interview, but on how well they exhibit the qualities of an elephant.

No trunk grows on Thanchanok's face.
But Thailand still gave her first place
In the beauty parade
Of the Jumbo brigade,
For her elegance, size, and her grace.

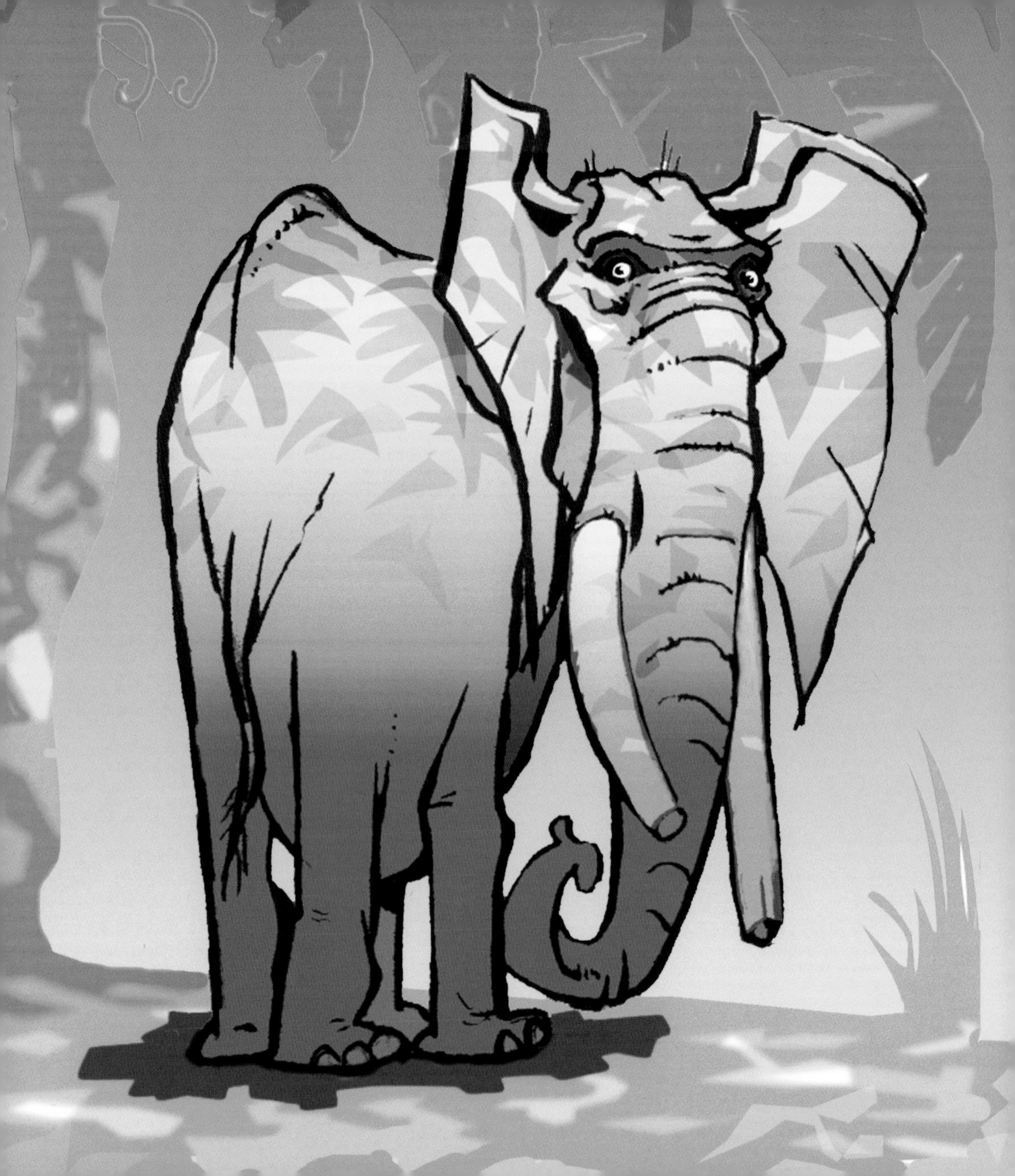

PACHYDERM PAPER MAKES A STATEMENT

Next time you receive an invitation to cocktails, your embossed card may just be published on paper made out of elephant dung. A company in Sri Lanka is now finding new ways to recycle elephant waste, turning it into a moneyspinner and a great conversation starter.

The company, Maximus (apparently named after the Asian elephant — *Elephas maximus*), stumbled upon the idea when their managing director read about a Kenyan game ranger who used elephant waste to make paper.

Maximus markets the paper — which costs slightly more than paper imported into Sri Lanka — to make greeting cards, menus, invitations and other fancy items.

Most of the users are pleasantly surprised, according to the Maximus managing director.

Moaned a Sri Lankan tusker, 'The pits,
This paper-pulp made from our shits!
   Next thing, believe me,
   There'll be ink from our pee,
Or white-out stuff based on our zits!'

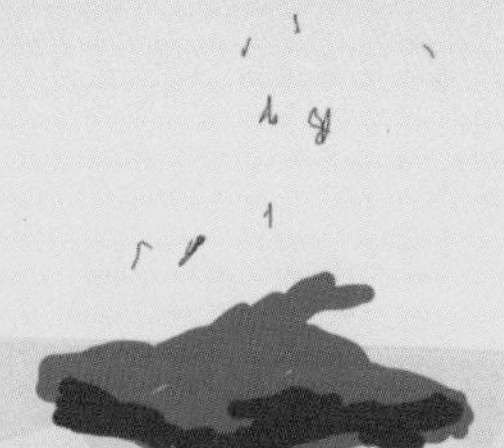

119

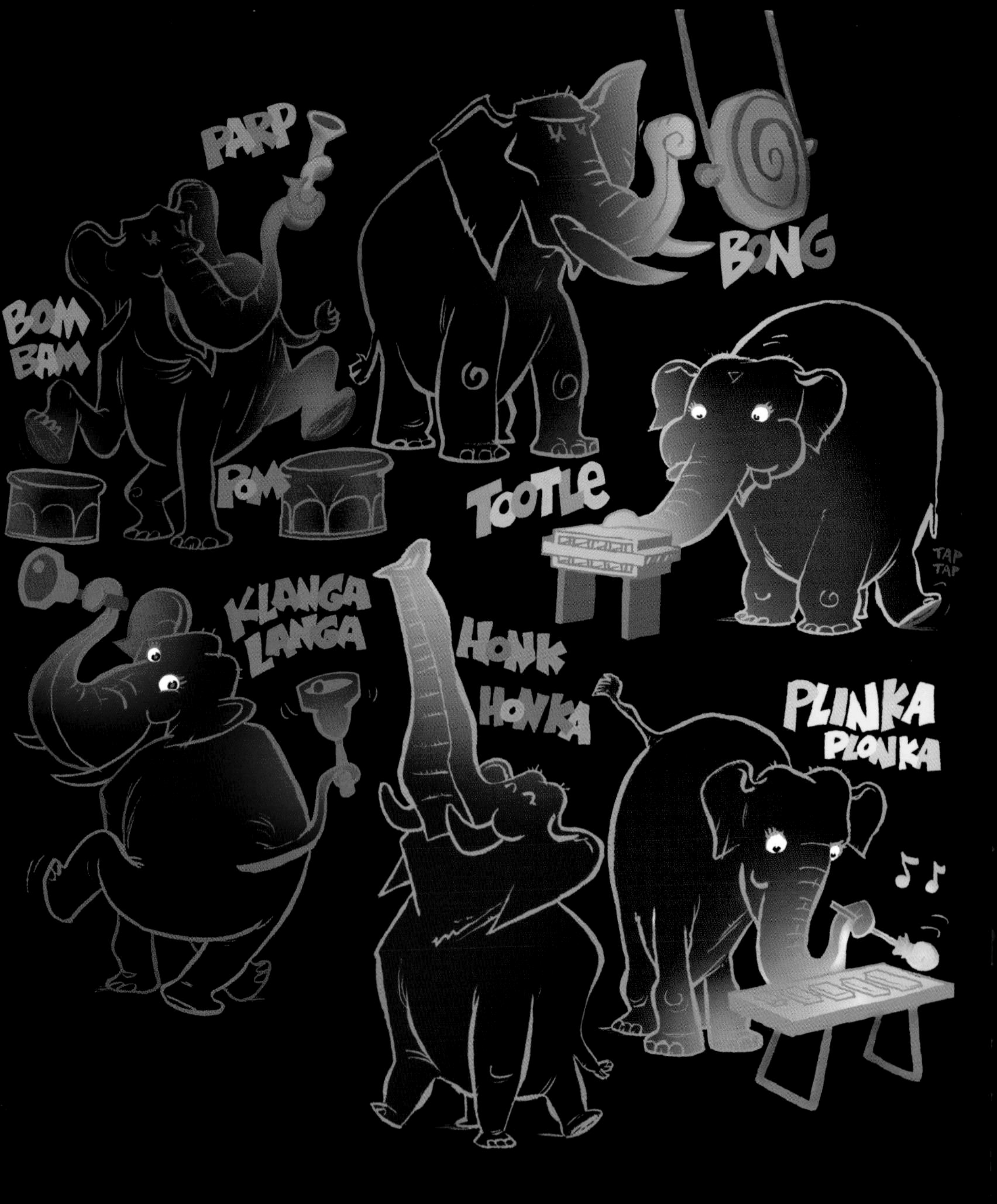
PARP
BONG
BOM BAM
POM
TOOTLE
TAP TAP
KLANGA LANGA
HONK HONKA
PLINKA PLONKA

THAI ELEPHANTS ON PARADE

Hear traditional Thai music, Beethoven's Pastoral Symphony, and even Hank Williams, all played by elephants. How is this possible? A human, like composer/performer Dave Soldier or Richard Lair of the Thai Elephant Conservation Center, cues the elephants when to enter and when to stop playing. The music that is made in between these signals is entirely up to the elephants.

The other way this works is the 'hocket' style, where each elephant plays one pitch of the scale on tuned angalungs. Composer/arranger/neuro-scientist David Soldier presents the new album by the planet's most potent passel of pachyderms, The Thai Elephant Orchestra. Really!

'These elephants play in fine fettle.
Their music's enough to unsettle
   My neurologist's mind,'
   Soldier mused; and opined,
'Casts a new light upon "Heavy Metal"!'

121

NEWS SOURCES

'Genes Reveal Africa's Elephants as Two Separate Species',
New York Times, 28 August 2001. By Andrew C. Revkin.
Sun Herald (Sydney), 2 September 2001.
Cf. *Columbus Dispatch*, Tuesday, 7 March 2006.

'Elephant Families Owe Their Success to Matriarchs' Age, Social
Skills', *National Geographic*, 19 April 2001. By Hillary Mayell.
http://news.nationalgeographic.com/news/2001/04/0419_el
ephantmamas.html.
Sydney Morning Herald, Weekend, 21–22 April 2001.
Cf. www.smh.com.au Sunday, 26 February 2006.

'Dumbo Needs Big Ears', BBC News, Wednesday, 14 March
2001, 20:44 GMT,
http://news.bbc.co.uk/1/hi/sci/tech/1220914.stm.

'Elephant Fossil Found in Kashmir', BBC News, Thursday,
7 September 2000, 03:17 GMT.

'Man and Other Animals', *The Guardian*, Saturday, 16 August
2003. By Jeremy Rifkin. (See also Prachett, Stewart and Cohen,
The Science of Discworld, p. 180.)

'Looking for Earth-shaking Clues to Elephant Communication',
Stanford Report, 1 June 2005, http://news-
service.stanford.edu/news/2005/june1/elephant-052505.html.

'How to Grab an Elephant's Ear', *Times*, 13 October 1999.

'Elephants Live in a Complex Society Bound Together by
Different Layers of Communication',
http://www.elephants.com/poole_address.htm,
November 2001.

'Professor Hopes to Clone Mammoth', Associated Press,
Saturday, 2 October 1999, 1:07 AM ET. By Jolyn Okamoto,
Associated Press Writer.

'Woolly Mammoth Resurrection, "Jurassic Park" Planned',
National Geographic, 8 April 2005. http://news.nationalgeo-
graphic.com/news/2005/04/0408_050408_woollymammoth.
html.
Cf. *Columbus Dispatch*, Tuesday, 7 March 2006.

'Zoo Touts Special Elephant Birth', Reuters, Monday,
29 November 1999, 9:29 PM ET. By Doug Johnson,
Associated Press Writer.

'Elephant-sized Fertility Treatment',
http://news.bbc.co.uk/hi/english/uk/newsid_1420000/14201
31.stm.
Cf. Reuters UK, Saturday, 4 March 2006.

'Breeding Elephants Can Invite a Ton of Trouble', *Washington
Post*, Monday, 29 March 1999. By Mary Jordan, Foreign
Service.

'Bull Elephants Fired for Frisky Behaviour', *Independent*, 3 August 2001. By P. B. Chandra in Jaipur.

'Thai Elephants Tie the Knot', BBC News, 14 February 2001, 16:47 GMT, http://news.bbc.co.uk/1/hi/world/asia-pacific/1169824.stm.

'Young Blood with a Taste for Trumpet', *Times*, 7 September 1999. By Russell Jenkins, North West Correspondent.

'Elephant Dies of Grief', BBC News, 5 May 1999.

'Mammoth Border Sneak', *San Antonio Express-News*, 30 January 2001. By Alison Gregor, Express-News Rio Grande Bureau.

'Heavyweight Trainer', http://www.afscme.org/publications/public_employee/1997/peso9706.htm.

'Zoo Used Electric Rods to Handle Elephants', *Independent*, 13 December 1999. By Harriet Tolputt.

'Kazakhs Soothe Fraught Elephant Nerves with Vodka', Reuters, Monday, 26 April 1999, 10:48 AM ET.

'Elephant Man of Zimbabwe Refuses to Follow the Herd', *Times*, 15 April 1999.

'Hungry Elephant Climbs to Safety', BBC News, Friday, 31 October 1997.

'Nagging Questions on the Wisdom of Zoos', *Christian Science Monitor*, 9 June 2005, http://www.csmonitor.com/2005/0609/p03s02-ussc.html.

'Thai Navy to Rescue Unemployed Elephants', *The Telegraph*, Tuesday, 8 May 2001, http://www.ananova.com/news/story/sm_284848.html?menu=.

'Minister Weighs Elephant-import Request', *Sydney Morning Herald*, Weekend, 2–3 June 2000.
Cf. ABC News Online, Tuesday, 3 May 2005 and *Sydney Morning Herald*, Weekend, 4–5 November 2006.

'Cruelty to Bereft Circus Elephant?', *Sydney Morning Herald*, Wednesday, 2 May 2000.

'Magistrate Rejects Elephant-cruelty Charge', *Sydney Morning Herald*, Weekend, 18-19 May 2002.

'Sport of Kings', *Bangkok Post*, 9 August 2001, http://www.bangkokpost.net/horizons/090801_Horizons16.html.
Cf. BBC, 6 December 2004, and *Washington Post*, Saturday, 19 August 2006, http://news.bbc.co.uk/1/hi/scotland/4073353.stm.

'Police Seize Elephants from Circus', Reuters, Friday, 27 October 2000, 8:24 AM ET.

'Microchips to Track Errant Elephants', Reuters, Friday, 3 September 1999, 7:31 AM ET.

'Elephants Evict Squatters', Reuters, Tuesday, 14 May 2002. *Sydney Morning Herald*, Thursday, 16 May 2002.

'Rampaging Elephants Add to Orissa's Woes', Independent, 16 November 1999. By Peter Popham in Delhi. Cf. *Decan Herald*, Tuesday, 5 June 2005 and New Delhi Television Ltd, Friday, 3 March 2006.

'Runaway Elephant Takes Over Publicity Stunt', Reuters, Wednesday, 26 May 1999, 11:29 AM ET.

'Elephants Pack Their Trunks and Say Goodbye to London Zoo', *Telegraph*, 1 November 2001. By Michael McCarthy, Environment Editor. *Union Jack* (America's National British Newspaper), December 2001.

'Vietnamese Elephants Trample Six People to Death', Australian Broadcasting Corporation, 7 December 1999.

'Crush Elephant had Violent Past', BBC News, Tuesday, 20 February 2001, 19:39 GMT, http://news.bbc.co.uk/1/hi/uk/1180988.stm.

'British Tourist Crushed in Elephant Attack', *Independent*, 5 October 1999.

'Journalist Trampled to Death by Elephant in China', Australian Broadcasting Corporation, 3 September 2001, 01:31:31 AEST.

'Elephant Tramples Man and Keeps the Corpse', Reuters, Tuesday, 2 January 2001, 10:15 AM ET, http://newsarchives.indiainfo.com/2000/12/31/31elephant.html.

'Elephants Eat Their Way to Equilibrium', BBC News, Thursday, 8 March 2001, http://news.bbc.co.uk/1/hi/sci/tech/1208970.stm.

'Confident Elephants Nudge into Nairobi', *Sydney Morning Herald*, Wednesday, 29 August 2001.

'Poachers have Created Breed of Tuskless Elephant', *Independent*, 19 June 2001. By Michael McCarthy, Environment Editor.

'Jumbos Jet in to Angola', BBC, Tuesday, 4 September 2001, 14:34 GMT.

'Thais Launch Campaign for Jumbo Wooden Leg', Australian Broadcasting Corporation, 24 August, 30 September, 5 October 1999.

'A Jumbo-sized Dilemma in Zambia', BBC News, Wednesday, 8 September 1999. By Ishbel Matheson in Lusaka.

'Surge in Zimbabwe Elephant Poaching', BBC News, Monday, 22 November 1999, http://news.bbc.co.uk/1/low/world/africa/531949.stm. Cf. Xinhua News, Wednesday, 22 March 2006.

'Elephants Hunted for Hair on Their Tails', Reuters, Monday, 8 February 1997, 11:16 AM ET.

'Elephant Forests will be Bugged', *Times*, 18 October 1999.

'Giuliani May Counter-sue Over New York Art Show', Reuters, Sunday, 3 October 1999, 4:12 PM ET. By Vicky Stamas.

'Elephant Painters', *Chiang Mai Mail*, 4 March 2005, http://chiangmai-mail.com/123/features.shtml. Cf. *Sydney Morning Herald*, Thursday, 21 June 2001 and CBS News, 14 February 2002, http://www.cbsnews.com/stories/2002/02/14/60minutes/main329450.shtml.

'Artful Elephants Rewarded', BBC News, Thursday, 21 February 2002, 12:34 GMT, http://news.bbc.co.uk/1/hi/entertainment/arts/1833814.stm. *Sydney Morning Herald*, Weekend, 23–24 February 2002.

'South African Game Park Offers Novel Memento', CNN, 14 July 1999.

'Thailand Crowns "Miss Jumbo Queen"', news.com.au, 2 May 2005, http://www.news.com.au/story/0,10117,15150643-13762,00.html.

'Pachyderm Paper Makes a Statement', BBC News, 5 July 2001, http://news.bbc.co.uk/hi/english/world/south_asia/newsid_1424000/1424155.stm. Cf. *Sri Lanka Daily News*, 17 May 2005, http://www.dailynews.lk/2005/05/17/bus07.htm.

'Thai Elephants on Parade', *Dusted Magazine*, 7 April 2005, http://www.dustedmagazine.com/reviews/2068. WNYC, 12 October, 2004, http://wnyc.org/shows/newsounds/episodes/10122004.

ABOUT THE AUTHOR:

R.J. Baker taught Latin, Greek and Ancient History for over 35 years in the Universities of Tasmania and New England, Australia, retiring from the latter as Associate Professor in 2001. He is presently an Honorary Fellow in the School of Classics, History and Religion there.

With his saucy old wit he may poke you,
In rhythm and rhyme he can joke you.
    In Limerick and Rome
    R.J. Baker is known
For poetry, both Haiku and Low-ku
JSB

ABOUT THE ILLUSTRATOR:

J.S. Baker has been in the animation industry since 1981, as an animator, character-designer and storyboard artist. He worked for a variety of studios in countries all over the world before settling in San Francisco in 1991. In his spare time he self-publishes comics, and threatens to one day write a children's book.

The message: 'Dad, I'm here to warn ya,
Not only will my pix adorn yer
    Text. But I'll quarrel
    With your Limerick laurel.
(Signed) Your son, SF, California.'

ABOUT THE ORIGINATOR:

Ada Cheung has a PhD in Ancient History from Monash University. She has since studied Law and presently works in the Department of Foreign Affairs and Trade.

Her interest in this is no mystery.
Ada cries, with a passion quite blistery,
    'Tuskers simply retain
    All their past in their brain;
Like my Law studies, and Ancient History!'

R.J. and J.S. Baker in earlier days, before capture by elephants.

First published 2007

Exisle Publishing Limited
'Moonrising', Narone Creek Road, Wollombi, NSW 2325, Australia
P.O. Box 60-490, Titirangi, Auckland 0642, New Zealand
www.exislepublishing.com

National Library of Australia Cataloguing-in-Publication Data

Baker, Robert J. (Robert John), 1939– .
Elephants in the news : pachyderms in limerick.

Bibliography.
ISBN 9780908988785.

1. Elephants – Poetry. 2. Limericks. 3. Australian wit
and humour. I. Baker, J. S. (James Stuart), 1964– . II. Title.

A821.4

10 9 8 7 6 5 4 3 2 1

Designed by www.saso.com.au
Typeset in Myriad Tilt 11/15 pt
Printed in China through Colorcraft Limited, Hong Kong